T0306025

MERCHANTS, BANKERS, GOVERNORS

**British Enterprise in Singapore and Malaya
1786–1920**

MERCHANTS, BANKERS, GOVERNORS

**British Enterprise in Singapore and Malaya
1786–1920**

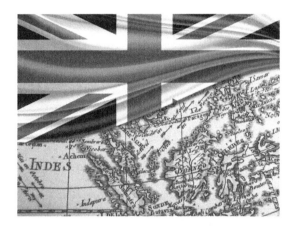

Peter J. Drake

World Scientific

NEW JERSEY · LONDON · SINGAPORE · BEIJING · SHANGHAI · HONG KONG · TAIPEI · CHENNAI · TOKYO

Published by

World Scientific Publishing Co. Pte. Ltd.
5 Toh Tuck Link, Singapore 596224
USA office: 27 Warren Street, Suite 401-402, Hackensack, NJ 07601
UK office: 57 Shelton Street, Covent Garden, London WC2H 9HE

Library of Congress Cataloging-in-Publication Data
Names: Drake, P. J. (Peter Joseph), author.
Title: Merchants, bankers, governors : British enterprise in Singapore and Malaya, 1786–1920 /
    by Peter J. Drake.
Description: New Jersey : World Scientific, [2017] | Includes bibliographical references and index.
Identifiers: LCCN 2017011670 | ISBN 9789813222410 (hardcover : alk. paper)
Subjects: LCSH: Great Britain--Commerce--Singapore--History. | Singapore--Commerce--
    Great Britain--History. | Great Britain--Commerce--Malaysia--Malaya--History. |
    Malaya--Commerce--Great Britain--History.
Classification: LCC HF3800.67.Z7 G73 2017 | DDC 382.0941/0595--dc23
LC record available at https://lccn.loc.gov/2017011670

British Library Cataloguing-in-Publication Data
A catalogue record for this book is available from the British Library.

Desk Editor: Jiang Yulin

Typeset by Stallion Press
Email: enquiries@stallionpress.com

Printed in Singapore

For Madeleine, Justin and Felicity,
who have waited
decades for their book.

Acknowledgements

Over the long gestation period of this book I have received much material support and encouragement from many institutions and colleagues, for which I am most grateful.

The Nuffield Foundation generously awarded me a Commonwealth Travelling Fellowship, which I held from August 1969 to October 1970 in the Institute of Commonwealth Studies, University of London. I was also made welcome and granted facilities in the neighbouring School of Oriental and African Studies of the University. The Nuffield Foundation also provided fine accommodation for my family. When I returned to London in 1984, the Nuffield Foundation again provided residential accommodation and the Institute of Commonwealth Studies an academic home again. The University of Melbourne and The University of New England each granted me study leave for these respective periods.

I owe special thanks to J. Gordon Menzies and George Rothery who took constant interest in my work and used their influence to open commercial doors for me in London. From the merchant firms and banks, I thank H.B. Roper-Caldbeck, Frank Man, T.M. Walker, A.E. Scott, John Wilson, J.H. Girling, K.G. Sinclair, J.H. Morris, T.B. Russell, T.B. Barlow, Keith Anderson and Ina Swain in London; and Eric Jennings, J.G. Gilmour and Sir Anthony Hayward in Singapore. Of particular mention is John Gullick who was a colonial civil servant in the Malay States before joining Guthrie & Co. in 1957; on his later retirement he continued to be a significant and productive scholar of Malaya and took much interest in this work.

In the academic world, I must first greatly thank John Drabble, with whom I have long enjoyed friendship and collaboration on our common interest in Malayan economic history. Chiang Hai Ding, Wong Lin Ken, C.D. (Jeremy) Cowan, Peter Lyon, Peter Ayre, Leslie Pressnell, Harold Luckham, Hal Hill and Gregg Huff deserve warm thanks for their advice and encouragement.

Susan Littler, Florence Harris and Joan Drake gave research assistance at different stages of the work. Jayne Carlon, Fiona Wilkinson and Kate McDowell typed various sections of the manuscript. I thank them all for their kind help.

Contents

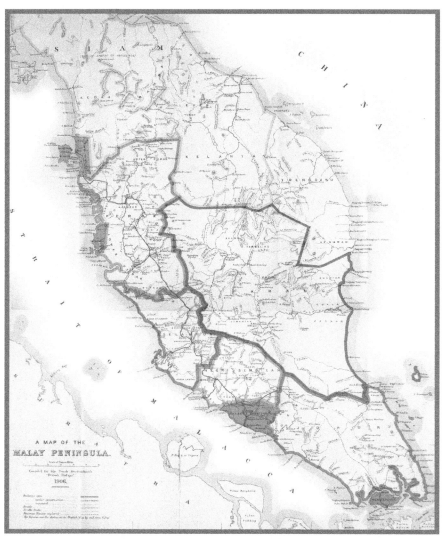

A map of the Malay Peninsula, compiled for Sir Frank Swettenham's *British Malaya: an account of the origin and progress of British influence in Malaya*, 1907. Downloaded from Flickr The Commons. No known copyright restrictions for the use of this image.

Preface

This is the story of British vision, zeal and drive in developing first Penang, then Singapore and finally the peninsular Malay States. Commerce and finance were initially paramount, the seeds having been planted by merchants, initially in the days of the East India Company and later by individual merchant firms, supported by credit from London. Not until the second quarter of the 19th century did government play a main role, and even then, it was chiefly by colonial officials on the ground. Government in London was lukewarm, and reluctant to be much involved with the Malay States, until driven by events in the middle of the century.

The great Straits Settlements merchant houses were "home-grown" and largely self-sufficient. They owed very little to prior direct investment or branching from the United Kingdom, India or Hong Kong. The basis of their success, and the vast capital they amassed, was Straits trade and investment in the Malayan peninsula, all based on exports of produce, tin and rubber.

The most striking feature of the merchants as class was not solidarity but competition, manifested in large numbers, low commission rates and frequent entrances, exits and amalgamations. The merchant firms were initially highly competitive, but by 1920 there had evolved mainly imperfect competition among a few large and dominant firms.

While the focus of this work is on British enterprise, I do not under-rate the contributions of the Malays, Indians and, especially, the Chinese to economic development. However, in the period under review, their activities were framed, steered and monitored by the British.

Peter J. Drake

Chapter 1

The Earliest Times: 1786–1850s

The Straits of Malacca are so situated as to permit whoever commands them to control seaborne trade between points East and West. In the days of sailing ships, and because of commercial and territorial rivalry among European powers at the time of the Napoleonic wars, Britain desired a base in the Straits in order to facilitate the then flourishing trade between British India and China, to compete with the Dutch (who were trying to maintain a monopoly of trade in the East Indies Archipelago) and to hold at bay any attempted invasion of the region by French commercial interests.

Britain's foothold in the region was gained in 1786, when the island of Penang was acquired by the British East India Co. Province Wellesley, across the water, was added to it in 1798. In 1805 the Penang jurisdiction was raised to the administrative status of fourth presidency of British India. The East India Co. acquired Singapore in 1819 and Malacca (as part of an intricate territorial deal with the Dutch) in 1824.

Much has been written about the foundation of Singapore and there is no need to repeat the tale here. Suffice it to note that the British had become very concerned about the possibility that the Dutch, who already had a firm hold on the Sunda Straits, might also gain command of the Straits of Malacca and thus control both channels of trade between China and Europe. Accordingly, the Governor-General of India, the Marquess of Hastings, instructed Sir Stamford Raffles to endeavour to establish a British station to command the eastern entrance to the Straits of Malacca;

he indicated that Rhio was perhaps the most suitable location, with Johore as a possibility if Rhio was unavailable. On finding Rhio already occupied by the Dutch, Raffles, interpreting his supplementary instructions rather freely, made an on-the-spot decision that the sparsely-inhabited island of Singapore was the best location and dropped anchor there on 28 January 1819, and within a short while made a treaty with the Malay Sultanate of Johore for the East India Co. to make and maintain a settlement on Singapore. The British merchants in Calcutta welcomed this outcome and their approbation supported Hastings in his support of Raffles (Collis, 1982, gives a concise and lively account of this period).

Penang, Singapore and Malacca were combined in 1826 into the Straits Settlements (S.S.), administered as a Presidency of India by the East India Co. until 1858, and then by the India Office until 1867. In that last year, the S.S. were separated from the India administration and given the status of Crown Colony under the control of the Colonial Office in London. British suzerainty in Malaya was confined to the S.S. until 1874, when the first political encroachment on the Malayan hinterland was made.

In the 90 or so years between 1786 and 1874, international commerce was essentially confined to entrepot trade between India, China and Europe which necessarily passed through the conveniently located Straits ports. "Entrepot" trade consists of import and re-export as distinct from importing foreign goods for local use and exporting local produce. "Transhipment", to be mentioned later, is a particular form of entrepot in which the imported commodities are not sold in the local entrepot market before re-export but simply transferred from one ship to another without any change in ownership of the goods. The trade of the S.S. also included the export of produce from the East Indies archipelago and the Malay Peninsula and a return flow of imports to those points. But the peninsula was sparsely settled and largely undeveloped until at least the 1850s. The S.S. initially waxed rich on the much larger entrepot trade.

The S.S. flourished under the umbrella of Britain's then powerful position in world trade and through a total commitment to the philosophy of free and unrestricted trade. Penang began under Francis Light's administration in 1786 as a free port, then uniquely so in Southeast Asia (Tregonning, 1965, p. 59); but in 1801, in a desperate search for government revenue, the administration of Sir George Leith imposed import and export taxes (*ibid.*, p. 63). However, these were abolished in 1826 after the unification of the S.S. ports as a single administrative unit.

The free trade policy of Singapore became the rule for the S.S. (*ibid.,* p. 72). Raffles, the founder of Singapore, had introduced a policy of free trade at the very beginning although, as Tregonning points out, not with any great enthusiasm for the principle. "It is not necessary at present to subject the trade of the port to any duties — it is yet inconsiderable; and it would be impolitic to incur the risk of obstructing its advancement by any measure of this nature" (*ibid.*, p. 154).

However, by 1822 Raffles was more positive in proclaiming:

Notice is hereby given, that with the exception of the regulations which may be established for restricting the consumption of opium and spirits, and the vice of gambling, and of such as may be established for the markets, and among the Chinese respecting the sale of pork, which are adopted as matters of policy for the general benefit of the whole community, the trade in all articles whatever is in every respect open and free to all persons without imposition of any kind whatever, the parties being at liberty to sell to whom they please without restriction.

That no person may plead ignorance of this regulation, the same is directed to be translated into the native languages and in a particular manner explained to the venders of attaps, timbers, spars, fire-wood, agar-agar, &c and published by beat of gong and affixed at the usual places for general information.

Given by me at Singapore, this 21st November, 1822.

(Signed)   *T.S. RAFFLES.*

Further, in a long letter instructing a small committee (Captain C.C. Davis, and Messrs George Bonham and Alex L. Johnston) to advise on the appropriation of land in Singapore, Raffles wrote, "it will be a primary object to secure to the mercantile community all the facilities which the natural advantages of the port afford." (Notices of Singapore, *Journal of the Indian Archipelago and Eastern Asia* (JIA), VII, 1853, p. 335 and VII, 1854, p. 102.)

Raffles' administrative successors found themselves — willy nilly — locked into the free trade policy, dictated from London and buttressed by the powerful merchants of Singapore.

By the late 18th century the East India Co. had become too cumbersome and bureaucratic an organisation to handle the fragmented river and coastal trade of the East Indies archipelago and of the mainland Malay, Burmese and Siamese states. This profitable and risky trade was conducted by the so-called "country traders" who plied the seas of Southeast Asia. These men worked the numerous small ports scattered around the islands; they formed loose trading associations, centred on Madras, and sailed under the British flag licensed by the company's authorities in Indian Presidency towns; but they were not members of the East India Co.

One such country trader was Light, employed as an agent of the Madras association of Jourdain, Sulivan and De Souza (Tregonning, 1965, pp. 7–9, 14). As early as 1771, Light had commended Penang as a desirable location for a trading settlement:

> *Withinside of Pulo Pinang is a fine clear channel of 7 and 14 fathoms through which a ship may work any time. I remember it was once your opinion that a House upon Pulo Pinang would be very useful; it would be extremely so because the Europe ships can easily stop there. There is plenty of wood, water and provisions there, they may be supplied with tin, pepper, beetlenut, rattans and birdsnests, and the Macao ships will be glad to stop there, and all other vessels passing through the Straits may be as easily supplied as at Malacca. Whether this would not suit the Company better than our Association I leave you to judge.* (Light to De Souza, 25 November 1771, quoted by Tregonning, 1965, p. 15.)

Light was appointed by the East India Co. 15 years later to be Superintendent of its newly acquired island of Penang. He retained his trading interests, in partnership from 1787 with James Scott as Scott & Co. (afterwards Brown & Co.), until his death in 1794. Scott apparently was to have sole charge of the firm, leaving Light free to administer the settlement so as to facilitate trade (Fielding, 1955, p. 38). It has been said that Light refrained from abusing "the combined position of Superintendent and principal merchant in Penang" (Skinner, 1895, p. 7). Light's own protestations to the Governor-General are also on record (Notices of Pinang, JIA, IV, 1850, pp. 652–653).

However, a more critical assessment of Light's merchant association with Scott and of the activities of Scott & Co. has been made (Stevens, 1929, pp. 379–385, 388). A contemporary critic, Captain Kyd the surveyor, claimed that Light and Scott constituted "so great a bar to all free enterprise that no commercial house or merchant of any credit had ever attempted to form an establishment" (quoted by Tregonning, 1965, p. 166). Fragmentary evidence lends some weight to that view. At the beginning of June 1793, Messrs James Scott & Co. accounted for 123,219 of a total of 182,702 Spanish dollars' value of goods and merchandise upon the island belonging to British subjects there; and for seven of a total of 10 vessels, and 131,073 of a total of 168,573 Spanish dollars' value of vessels and cargoes belonging to British inhabitants of the island, at sea in the Straits of Malacca and eastward (JIA, IV, 1850, p. 662).

Members of the East India Co.'s marine service were allowed, subject to some restrictions, from 1796 to trade on their own accounts and many did so. In 1813, the trade of India was thrown open to private traders and it became more attractive for East India Co. mariners to work independently than to remain in the Co.'s service, where pay was now fixed and the privilege of private trading as a sideline abolished (Cunyngham-Brown, 1971, pp. 16, 38). The opening of the India trade also attracted new merchants to the East, as did the British occupation of Java in 1811 and the abolition of the East India Co.'s monopoly of trade with China in 1833. From then on, the eastern trade was wide open to all comers.

In 1819 James Matheson, on route to China, had written:

I have formed the highest opinion of Singapore as a place of trade.... As yet, however, no trade can be carried on to any great extent there being no merchants to deal with; but this is a disadvantage which, as there are no duties or port charges, will soon vanish. (Quoted by Greenberg, 1951, p. 97.)

The deficiency was indeed soon remedied. Within very few years after its foundation, Singapore outstripped the other two ports in importance as Table 1 shows. Inevitably, therefore, the emphasis remained on Singapore

Table 1.   Total Trade (Exports and Imports) (£'000s).

Year	Singapore	Penang	Malacca
1825	2,610	1,115	318
1833	3,748	867	162
1843	5,548	1,022	157
1850	5,637	1,645	439
1853	6,515	1,687	517

Sources: Cameron, 1965, p. 179; Winstedt, 1966, p. 61.

right up to the last quarter of the 19th century, when merchant firms and banks at last felt the need for permanent and substantial representation on the Malay peninsula.

In 1827 the European population in Singapore numbered 94, in 1833 they were 119 and by 1841 about 300. At the census of 1845, the European population was enumerated at 336, in 1849 at 360 and in 1860 at 466 of whom 271 were adult British males (Turnbull, 1969, p. 13). Many of these men were principals or employees of merchant firms. Those firms numbered 14 in 1827 (Wong, 1960, p. 167) and 17 in 1834 (listed in Table 2 and including many of the pioneering merchants) and 20 a year later (Earl, 1971, p. 415).

The only available contemporary remarks about the early British merchants are by John Crawfurd (in 1824 the Resident of Singapore), T.J. Newbold (an army officer who served in the S.S. in 1832–1835) and G.W. Earl (who resided temporarily in Singapore in 1833–1834). Crawfurd recorded in his General Report on Singapore dated 9 January 1824: "There are 12 European firms, either agents of or connected with good London or Calcutta houses, some have branches at Batavia, and not one can be called an adventurer." (Notices of Singapore, JIA, IX, 1855, p. 468.)

Newbold wrote: "Few of the European merchants at Singapore transact business on their own account, being mostly agents for European houses." (Newbold, 1971, p. 352.)

Earl wrote: "The British merchants are chiefly commission agents, who receive consignments of goods from merchants in Great Britain and

Table 2.   List of Merchant Firms in Singapore by 1834 Showing the Years in Which They Were Founded.

1. A.L. Johnston & Co., 1819 or 1820
2. Guthrie & Co., 1821
3. George Armstrong & Co., 1822
4. John Purvis & Co., 1822
5. Syme & Co., 1823
6. Spottiswoode & Connolly, 1824
7. Jose D'Almeida & Sons, 1825
8. Maclaine Fraser & Co., 1825
9. Crane Bros., 1825
10. Maxwell & Co., existing by 1827
11. Morgan Hunter & Co., existing by 1827
12. Napier, Scott & Co., existing by 1827*
13. Thomas & Co., existing by 1827
14. Ker, Rawson & Co., 1828
15. Boustead & Co., 1830
16. Hamilton, Gray & Co., 1832
17. Shaw, Whitehead & Co., 1834

* But apparently founded in 1819.
Source: Loh, 1958, p. 64.

make returns in oriental produce purchased in the settlement." (Earl, 1971, p. 416.)

It cannot be inferred from these observations that the merchant firms were mere subsidiaries or extensions of London firms or Calcutta agency houses. On the contrary, it seems that the Straits merchants were mostly independent individuals, often teaming together in small partnerships. They did indeed take goods on consignment from British exporters; some had split off from older British merchant firms at home or in the colonies; and some had connections to agency houses in India, especially in the earliest days when the East India Co. was still powerful. But it would be wrong to think of the Straits firms as dependent branches of firms based elsewhere. The available evidence of a few important firms supports this view.

David Napier and Charles Scott set up business in 1819 as Napier, Scott & Co, said to be the first firm in Singapore (Cunyngham-Brown, 1971, p. 27).

A.L. Johnston, formerly an East India Co. mariner, settled in Singapore in 1819 as a private trader and founded the firm which bore his name (Turnbull, 1969, p. 24; Loh, 1958, p. 7).

Alexander Guthrie arrived in Singapore in 1820 as the resident partner of the small Capetown firm of Messrs Harrington & Co. Guthrie and Harrington dissolved the partnership in November 1823, and in February 1824 the partnership of Guthrie and Clark was established, retaining Guthrie's existing association with W.J. Burnie & Co. of London as consignors. The firm became Guthrie & Co. in 1833 (Cunyngham-Brown, 1971, pp. 26, 37, 58).

John Purvis came to Singapore from Canton in 1822 and established his own firm (Turnbull, 1969, p. 29).

T.O. Crane arrived unintentionally in Singapore in 1825, beginning in business as an auctioneer and land agent before becoming a merchant (Loh, 1958, pp. 10–11).

Paterson, Simons & Co., 1858, descended (via Ker, Rawson & Co., 1828) from the London and Liverpool merchant firm Rawson, Holdsworth & Co. (unauthenticated typescript, n.d., from Paterson, Simons & Co.).

Edward Boustead, who had formerly been in the China trade, arrived in Singapore in 1828 to manage the firm of Robert Wise & Co. (of which no record remains). Boustead founded his own firm in 1830 (Loh, 1958, p. 11).

An important figure in early Singapore was Dr Joze d'Almeida who first established a medical practice in the city around 1825. He was drawn into the merchant business as a result of effectively promoting the sale of cargo of Portuguese and Spanish ships which were laid up, as a result of monsoons, in Singapore harbour for several months. The success of this selling venture led him to establish a merchant firm which by the time of his death in 1850 was one of the great firms in Singapore (Loh, 1958, p. 10; see also the introduction by C.M. Turnbull in Earl, 1971).

The local prominence of the merchant community is reflected in the fact that at least 11 and probably all 15 of the listed "gentlemen resident at Singapore who are considered competent to act as Magistrates" and were so proclaimed on 1 February 1823, were British merchants (Notices of Singapore, JIA, IX, pp. 336, 469).

There is no evidence that the early merchants brought much personal capital with them, a view endorsed by Loh (1958, p. 15). Indeed, fragments point in the opposite direction. For example, the Inspector of the Chartered Bank wrote in 1866 that "the Singapore people are not as a rule rich and are exceedingly timorous of their little means" (Chartered Bank Inspector's Letter Book, authentic typescript of original since destroyed).

Singapore's mercantile business was not an outlet for long-term investment capital (direct or portfolio) from Britain. The Straits merchant firms were, however, a funnel for trade credit originating in Britain; and it was this short-term credit which enabled the merchants to do a business of value well above the total of their own resources.

Trade credit from suppliers in Britain was not alone sufficient: it was also necessary for the merchants to have contacts and financial dealings with numerous Chinese and other Asian traders and producers in the Straits and, after the advent of banks in the Straits ports in the 1840s, frequent recourse to the banks for discounting of bills of exchange and promissory notes or for overdraft accommodation. There was a crucial dependence between British and Asian traders in the Straits ports, because each had something that the other lacked but needed. The British alone possessed the knowledge of — and connections and lines of credit with — suppliers, buyers, shippers and insurers based in the United Kingdom; the Asians alone had penetrated the hinterland and the archipelago whence went imports and came produce.

According to Earl's contemporary account:

[The British merchants] *rarely engage in commercial speculations with the islands in the Archipelago. The Europeans have very little direct commercial intercourse with the traders who visit the port, as their goods are purchased by the Chinese, who have a better acquaintance with the natives, and have patience enough to go into all the necessary details of bargaining and weighing the goods. When a European merchant wishes to make a shipment of produce to England, he visits the bazaar, and purchases the articles he requires from the Chinese in exchange for others which have been consigned to him.* (Earl, 1971, p. 416.)

The cornerstone of the mercantile business was the entrepot nature of the Straits trade. In the beginning, the trade of the Straits ports was based to a large extent on the mere transhipment of goods between East and West in order to evade the monopoly of the East India Co. on direct trade between China and Europe.

The revival of private trade between Europe and the East using Singapore as a port of transhipment attracted many European merchants to the new settlement. These merchants were paid a commission ranging from ½% to 1% for supervising the process of transhipment (Loh, 1958, p. 5).

Some indication of the importance of Singapore as a point of transhipment can be gained from the fact that the transhipments in the port involved almost one quarter of each of the export and import trade of India in 1828–1829, valued respectively at £8.7 million and £8.25 million (Sardesai, 1977, p. 50).

As well as actual transfers by merchants of goods between ships in Singapore, a legal loophole was exploited before 1833 in the name of transhipment:

> *Cargo taken aboard at Lintin or Macao was landed in Singapore; fresh bills of lading were made out to London consignees, and the cargo taken aboard again on the same ship, which then proceeded to England. By this legal fiction, a serious inroad into the East India Company's monopoly of the Anglo-Chinese trade was made possible.* (Greenberg, 1951, p. 97.)

Although the East India Co.'s China monopoly was abolished in 1833, Straits entrepot trade continued to flourish, so great was Singapore's natural advantage of location as both the crossroads of trade between Europe, the Indian Empire and China, and the hub of regional trade within Southeast Asia.

The flavour of Singapore's trade is captured in a description of the early activities of Alexander Guthrie, founder of the great firm which still bears his name: "to ship out the spices, nutmegs and pepper of the East and bring in the knives of Sheffield, the cotton goods of Lancashire and the other substantial exports of Victorian England" (*Straits Times*, quoted in Loh, 1958, p. 8). Table 3 shows the components of trade classified by main trading partners, while Table 4 reveals the broad geographical pattern of Singapore's trade up to 1861. Underlying the growing importance

Table 3. Trade of Singapore in the 1830s.

Main Trading Partners; Countries Ranked in Order of Value	Components of the Trade	
	Imports From	**Exports To**
China	Tea, napkins, piece goods, sugar-candy, china and copperware, gold and silver thread, raw silk, cassia, tobacco, specie.	British cottons and woollens cloth, opium, betel nut, ebony, edible birds' nests, seaweed, tin, pepper.
India and Ceylon	Opium, rice, saltpetre, ebony, cotton, Indian piece goods, arrack, cordage.	Tin, gold, nankin, chinaware, pepper, gambier, spices.
Great Britain	Woollen piece goods, cotton twist, iron, arms, gunpowder, wines, manufactures in great variety.	Antimony, tin, tea, gold, cassia, coffee, sugar, raw silk, hides, ivory, tortoise shell, beeswax, mother of pearl.
Java	European piece goods (excess stock from the Batavia market), *beche de mer*, edible birds' nests, gold, indigo, rice, rattans, spices, benjamin, brass and copper ware, tin, tobacco, sandalwood, arrack and other spirits.	Piece goods from India, China and Europe, nankin, iron, opium, raw silk, wheat, china and iron ware, cordage, gunnies, saltpetre.
Malay Peninsula (east)	Gold, tin, pepper, silk and cotton Malay cloths, sugar, rattans.	Rice, tobacco, opium, salt, salt-fish, arms, iron tools, agricultural implements, piece goods, cotton twist.
Malay Peninsula (west)	Beeswax, elephant's teeth, ebony, hides, rattans, sago, cattle, poultry, fruit, vegetables.	Rice, tobacco, opium, salt, salt-fish, arms, iron tools, agricultural implements, piece goods, cotton twist.

(*Continued*)

Table 3. (*Continued*)

Main Trading Partners; Countries Ranked in Order of Value	Components of the Trade	
	Imports From	Exports To
Siam	Rice, sugar, ivory, oil, salt, iron pans, wood.	British and Indian piece goods, opium, woollen cloths, cotton twist, beeswax, betel nut, ebony, steel, iron, lead, rattans.
Other East Indies islands	Gold, ebony, ivory, camphor, tin, mother of pearl, pearls, benjamin, tortoise shells, birds' plumes, diamonds, birds of paradise, beeswax, *beche de mer*, coffee, spice, Maccassar and other oils, pepper, rice, edible birds' nests, spices, tobacco, wood, antimony.	Piece goods from Britain, India and Malaya, woollens, rice, iron, brass, earthen and china ware, opium salt, raw silk, tobacco, gunpowder, cotton twist, iron, steel iron tools, agricultural implements.

Lesser value trade conducted with Cochin China, Continental Europe, Mauritius, Cape Colony, New South Wales, Arabia, United States.

Source: Abridged from Newbold, 1839, pp. 252–259. A detailed statement of imports and exports by commodity and by value for each of the three Straits Settlements for the year 1828–1829 can be found as a table after p. 386 of Begbie, 1834, reprinted 1967.

Table 4. Singapore's Trade (in '000s of Dollars).

Fiscal Year	Total Value	Of Which From (Imports) or To (Exports)				
		UK	India	China	Archipelago	Southeast Asia
	Imports					
1825–26	6,269	856	957	1,690	390	676
1830–31	8,910	1,162	1,369	2,790	1,709	2,310
1835–36	7,368	1,112	1,490	595	1,779	2,382
1840–41	14,158	2,914	4,553	1,613	2,158	3,106
1845–46	12,816	3,160	2,513	1,229	1,878	2,973
1850–51	13,744	2,730	2,377	1,071	1,753	3,163
1855–56	22,904	4,164	3,809	2,783	2,724	4,694
1860–61	25,812	10,029	1,691	2,092	3,999	7,170
	Exports					
1825–26	5,358	1,800	397	744	146	363
1830–31	8,679	3,470	653	867	1,236	1,996
1835–36	6,962	869	564	1,050	1,436	2,303
1840–41	11,908	2,193	1,074	2,772	1,328	2,441
1845–46	10,498	977	2,421	2,420	1,570	2,801
1850–51	11,366	1,129	1,265	2,243	1,327	2,653
1855–56	19,698	1,937	1,209	3,271	2,472	4,153
1860–61	18,654	2,980	1,106	3,319	3,334	6,751

Source: Sardesai (1977, pp. 52–53).

of trade with the Malay peninsula, the East Indies Archipelago and the rest of Southeast Asia, and the relative decline of Indian trade, were the growth of world markets for "Straits produce" and the trade stimulus from Dutch and French extensions into the then East Indies and Cochin China. The restrictive tariff policies practised by the Dutch and French, however, tended to drive much new trade illicitly to Singapore (Sardesai, 1977, pp. 56–59).

The entrepot style of Singapore's trade married nicely to the bartering of British manufactures against Eastern produce, thus minimising the need of all parties to hold large cash balances or investment in stocks. To this style of trade, the consignment system was also well-suited. Manufactures from Britain, especially cotton and woollen piece goods, were consigned to merchants in Singapore and Penang to be sold on commission. The consignment was usually organised not by the manufacturer but by a consigning firm in Britain. (For example, W. & J. Burnie & Co. of London were consignors for Guthrie.) In the early days, the consignments were not to order from the Straits but were sent as surplus stock for disposal. The consignors in Britain commonly took in return the Straits merchant's bill of exchange, payable six months later, i.e., a "long" bill (Loh, 1958, p. 16). Should the consignor not wish to hold the bill until the date of its maturity, he could discount it, for time and/or risk, with a bank in Britain. Sometimes consignments were promptly acquitted by payment in specie or gold dust or by return shipments of Eastern produce (Newbold, 1971, p. 350). It seems, however, that most shipments were covered by bills drawn upon Straits importers.

When goods arrived at a Straits port, the consignments were broken down and advanced in smaller portions and on credit to Asian traders, predominantly Chinese. Indians retained most of the trade with India but the competitive Chinese destroyed other Asian middlemen (Wong, 1978, p. 83). The so-called "long credit" which the merchant firms received from British exporters was passed on as shorter trade credit, usually unsecured, to Chinese distributors. To a very considerable extent, physical barter then came into play — the Chinese distributors often discharged their debts by rendering to the European merchants local produce, obtained "outport" or "outstation" which the merchants in due course exported to Europe, or to America, using the sale proceeds, *inter alia*, to discharge their bill of exchange obligations arising from their imports.

In the early days, the trade of Singapore was wholly barter, owing to some extent to a scarcity of specie currency (coin) in the port:

> *In considering the extent of the trade at Singapore, rated not in goods but in money, some reference must be made to the peculiar method in which all commercial dealings are conducted; the unceasing drain of specie leaves not any scarcely in the place. Specie, therefore, never enters into any common transaction. All goods are disposed of on credit,*

generally for two months, and to intermediate native Chinese merchants,
and those at the expiration of the period deliver in return not money, but
articles of Straits produce adapted to the return cargo.... (Fullerton,
Chief Resident, S.S., 1830, quoted in Wright and Cartwright, 1908. See
also Wong, 1960, p. 163.)

Currency was indeed scarce, but the shortage of cash should not be
allowed to obscure the basic suitability of barter to the trade of the
Straits ports, because imports and exports were reasonably well bal-
anced. The barter practices dovetailed neatly with the shipping trade:
ships emptied in Singapore of European manufactures could be refilled
for the return journey to Europe with "Straits produce", a loose term
embracing all the metals, foodstuffs, spices, dyes, wood, etc., produced
in the Straits, the Malay Peninsula, the East Indies archipelago and
Siam. It must be remembered that these financial and shipping practices
were simply the detailed manifestation of the over-riding, two-way
nature of the entrepot trade: fundamentally, the Straits ports provided for
the East–West exchange of Straits produce and China goods against the
manufactures of Europe and various products of India, notably including
opium.

For these reasons, barter held on well into the 20th century. The
Report of the 1933–34 Trade Commission described it as follows: "The
two sides of the trade are complementary; the produce pays for the manufactures, and the machinery of collection is closely interlocked with that
of distribution...." (Quoted by Wong, 1978, p. 82.)

The European merchant firms passed goods on credit to the Straits
Chinese distributors who "... in turn, extended the credit structure to the
rest of Southeast Asia, on a clan, kith and kin basis.... The small trader
was directly financed by the Chinese dealer, who received in payment
Straits produce for Western imports sold to him...." (Wong, 1978, p. 83.)

A British Administration Report immediately after World War II
described the final pieces of a trade structure that had lasted for more than
a century:

The outport dealer thereafter requires to liquidate the debt he has
incurred in Singapore, and does so by delivery to that market of the

produce that he has acquired in the course of disposing of his stock of manufactured goods. Credit is given throughout the range of intermediaries, and it is the final credit stage — the pledging of his crop by the peasant for goods obtained from the village trader, who in turn has obligations towards the dealer who supplied him — ensures the despatch of an outport crop to Singapore. (Quoted in Wong, 1978, p. 84.)

The European merchant firms originally gave two months' credit to the Chinese distributors but the most common period soon became three months and was often stretched to six. The merchant firms ran risks of default when they gave goods on credit to the Chinese middlemen. Default was common and the merchants frequently attempted to make collective credit rules designed to minimise defaults. Now and then they also sought to agree to obtain cash, rather than produce, settlements from the Chinese. The earliest record of such a mercantile agreement was in 1835 (Loh, 1958, p. 17; Wong, 1960, p. 163), but then, as on many later occasions, agreement was of little avail. The problem of default recurred constantly, and will be discussed as appropriate in later chapters.

By and large the Chinese middlemen really traded on the capital of the Europeans and made repayments "according to the pressure exerted by the European firms" (Wong, 1960, p. 163). The Chinese even at times took European goods and sold them below cost in Penang for cash, in order to get capital for trade with the Bugis (Turnbull, 1972, p. 181; Wong, 1960, pp. 163–164). If the ventures failed, the European merchant was never paid. Sometimes he was not paid even after successful trading by the Chinese because some of them absconded. The extension to the Straits in 1848 of the Insolvent Law of India, with its protracted legal machinery for claiming upon the property of a defaulter, merely increased the ease with which defaulters could evade their creditors (Wong, 1960, pp. 164–165), and "there were cases of Chinese sending their profits to China and then declaring themselves bankrupt" (Turnbull, 1972, p. 181).

The European merchants could not do without the Chinese. Wong notes the failure of European efforts to displace the Chinese middlemen in the 1860s — the extended and intricate webs of local distribution, collection and credit were irreplaceable (Wong, 1978, p. 83). And since the Chinese seldom had sufficient capital, the Europeans inevitably had to

Table 5. Number of Merchants and Value of Trade.

Year	Number of Merchant Firms (Principally European) Listed in the Singapore Directory	Total Value of Trade, Exports Plus Imports $m	Average Value of Trade per Firm $m
	(a)[1]	(b)[2]	(c) = (b)/(a)
1827	14	13.1	0.935
1846	36	25.7	0.713
1855	36	32.8	0.911
1858	44	53.0	1.204
1864	52	51.8	0.996
1867	60	55.1	0.918
1870	62	58.8	0.948

[1] Wong, 1960, p. 167.

[2] Wong, 1978, p. 57.

fund Chinese activities. The European merchants not only stood the risks with Chinese middlemen but were also vulnerable to competition from newcomers of their own kind. Anyone who could get a line of trade credit from a supplier in Britain could get a foothold in the import trade. Constant pressures of this nature led many merchants into overtrading and the risky extension of credit to Chinese middlemen. Some statistics about the numbers of merchants in Singapore and the value of the trade there illustrate how quickly the trade was cut up by competition. Table 5 suggests that when the average value of annual turnover rose new firms entered and competed it down. However, these figures must be handled with care. The numbers of firms and of merchants are neither equal nor proportional; some firms did more business than others; the definition of firms is not clear cut; and it cannot be assumed that all recorded trade went through the hands of firms listed in the Singapore Directory.

The European merchant structure also changed frequently, for quite natural reasons, through amalgamations, and by the admission of new partners and the retirement of old ones. The *Straits Times* in 1867 described European mercantile life as "a long drudgery which men enter upon in their youth and leave in their old age" (Quoted by Turnbull, 1972,

p. 31). Turnbull says that they mostly retired with "only a modest competence", and she quotes the *Singapore Free Press* in 1860 as saying that, for the individual European merchant, the Singapore entrepot trade was "only very moderately prosperous and at times the very reverse" (*ibid.*).

Whilst in later years the improvements in transport and communications, and the growth of the London end of the mercantile business, meant that merchants could and did move more frequently between Britain and the Straits, for the most of the 19th century it was indeed a life sentence in the East. One cannot so readily agree that the European merchants enjoyed merely "moderate" prosperity or "modest" competence, however those words may be defined. No doubt those men who never rose above the level of employee amassed little capital, although for the years of their working lives they almost certainly lived better than they would have done from comparable white-collar jobs at home. The principals or partners of the firms, however, seem to have done quite well. Certainly those of Guthries and Bousteads capitalised themselves to the extent of owning London houses and country estates in the UK, to say nothing of their vestigial post-retirement interests in their firms and real estate in the Straits or on the Malay peninsula. One cannot assume that the same went for all the members of all firms, but the probability of becoming wealthy was always possible when one really good trading year could set a man up for life.

Two broader aspects of merchant activity deserve mention at this stage. As a collective group, the merchants engaged, as occasion demanded, in political lobbying; and they formed Chambers of Commerce. These things were interrelated.

The interplay of political and trade considerations was strong in the infant S.S. as the livelihood of the merchants was often dependent on political decisions. To some extent the merchants had always been able to exert influence through legal channels. As mentioned earlier, in February 1823 a regulation to establish a Provisional Magistracy named 15 residents, including at least a dozen known merchants, as Magistrates. Subsequently, a merchant voice in public affairs was obtained through the system of Grand Jury, of which there was one in each Settlement.

The Grand Jury was a body composed of important citizens but with undefined authority. In addition to court attendance and inspection and reporting responsibilities, the Grand Jury was permitted:

> *... to make a Presentment on any subject of public interest they deemed fit, including matters which would normally have been the responsibility of the Legislative Council and representative municipal authorities, had these existed.* (Turnbull, 1969, p. 20ff., from which the following text draws substantially.)

As well as pronouncing on such municipal matters as town drainage, dirt and noise in the streets, fire hazards and so on, the Grand Jury provided an outlet for criticism of government and indeed of Governors. However, it was not much more than an outlet; and as the Jury's powerlessness was appreciated, the merchants came to grudge the time spent in its service. The Singapore Grand Jury became quiescent under the astute and benevolent rule of Governor Orfeur Cavenagh (1859–1867), and in 1860 it disclaimed any right to be regarded as representative of the public.

Outside the Grand Jury, but with obvious influence on it, were public meetings. These were held as occasion demanded and were also concerned with both municipal and wider political issues. The meetings provided a natural opportunity to express dissent from official views and the deliberations of such meetings often gave rise to petitions which were presented to the authorities and published in the local press. The local newspapers played an important role in sustaining freedom of expression and political activity, and in forming public opinion. A number of the merchant and professional classes — notably Edward Boustead, William Napier, Abraham and James Logan, James Cameron and Robin Woods — were involved in the *Singapore Free Press*, the *Penang Gazette* and the *Straits Times* (Turnbull, 1972, pp. 25–7, 130–3):

> *The heyday of the public meetings came in the 1850s when in the hands of a small minority, with the constant backing of the Straits Times and generally with support from the Free Press, these gatherings and the politicians they produced became a troublesome and effective opposition to the government.* (Turnbull, 1969, p. 27.)

Moreover, the public meetings were by no means confined to European settlers but also captured the opinions and the services of influential Asians.

Out of the public meetings grew agitation for constitutional reform. Since at least the 1830s there had been sporadic talk about removing the S.S. from the control of India and giving them Crown Colony status. In 1857 — the population being agitated and anxious by fears of possible local uprisings in the wake of the Indian Mutiny — a public meeting in Singapore was called by the European merchants and it resolved, among other things, to petition London for direct rule. The petition went only from Singapore; a similar public meeting in Penang declined to support the Singapore demands. The Singapore petition was received favourably by the House of Commons, although it took a further 10 years for the idea of Crown Colony status for the S.S. to be translated into reality (Turnbull, 1977, pp. 70–5). The long delay was due essentially to London's doubts about the financial viability of the colony on a self-supporting basis. The East India Co., having found the S.S. burdensome, especially after the 1833 loss of its monopoly in the China trade, ran a lean and cheap administration in the Straits. The transfer of authority from the East India Co. to the India Office in 1858 did not change the nature of the problem.

It is important to realise that Singapore was not the primary centre of the S.S. in the early years after their formation in 1826. Penang was the capital until 1833, when capital status was transferred to Singapore. However, the rapid growth of Singapore as an entrepot ran ahead of governance developments, quickly put paid to any expansion of Malacca and drew away much of the trade of Penang. Singapore's superior geographic location attracted the merchants and financiers who provided the framework for the entrepot trade and made Singapore the most prosperous of the British establishments in the Straits. Nonetheless, Penang's long-established mercantile community remained in place and sought to protect its interests against both interference from government and competition from Singapore. It is particularly interesting that in February 1837 first Penang and then Singapore each formed a Chamber of Commerce to represent local mercantile viewpoints to government and set down norms for merchant commerce:

The Penang Chamber of Commerce and Agriculture is formed for the protection of the General interests of the trade of the Settlement, for collecting and classifying mercantile information, for establishing a Court of Arbitration to adjust commercial differences which may be referred to it, and for communicating with the public authorities on all subjects affecting the common good. (Quoted in Gale, 1987, p. 39, from which this section draws substantially.)

The Singapore Chamber set down the same aims in almost identical words. The Singapore Chamber of Commerce also was established in 1837, largely on the initiative of Edward Boustead, who had come to Singapore from China and founded Boustead & Co. around 1830 and who also had been for a time the editor of the *Singapore Chronicle.* The Chamber was open to businessmen of all races; its first committee included Europeans, Chinese, Eurasians, Arabs and Americans, and was presided over by the leading merchant A.L. Johnston.

The initial membership of the Penang Chamber and of its Committee of Management reflected both the several ethnic groups engaged in Penang commerce and the overall leadership by British merchants. The three executive officers were all British but the remaining six members were variously Chinese, Arab/Malay and Indian.

The Penang Chamber's first concern was about Dutch aggression in the coastal trading ports of Sumatra and the possible consequences of such "mischief" on the trade of the S.S. There was a particular fear in 1849 of extension of Java's tariff to the independent territories of Sumatra, to the detriment of free trade in coffee. The Chamber indirectly sought action from London but, although tension persisted between the mercantile community and the Dutch authorities, the British government refused to intervene. The Dutch had withdrawn from Sumatra in 1842 but their interest in that territory was rekindled and a treaty was concluded with Siak in 1858. The Penang and Singapore Chambers of Commerce both protested until in 1865 Governor Cavenagh supported a petition by the Penang merchants protesting at Dutch activities in Sumatra. Finally, in 1871, an Anglo-Dutch Treaty permitted British traders to operate freely in Sumatra under Dutch rule.

Although the Penang and Singapore Chambers operated on like terms and usually co-operatively, the Penang merchants became increasingly jealous and resentful of Singapore's prosperity. They declined to support the Transfer movement, which was strongly advocated in Singapore. After the Crown Colony was established in 1867, the Penang Chamber remained dissatisfied. In 1872, its Chairman made a speech demanding that Penang be given separate governance with its own Legislative Council. Much of the dissatisfaction stemmed from the Penang perception that Singapore got more than its fair share of public works and revenue. Despite various concessions granted to Penang by the Straits government, resentment against Singapore continued to the end of the century.

The Penang and Singapore Chambers achieved considerable successes when they acted jointly. For example, public meetings mounted by the Chambers in both cities opposed and thwarted the attempt by the Indian authorities to impose rupee coinage in the Straits (of which more in the next chapter). Similar joint petitions blocked the Governor's 1856 attempt to increase port dues. Finally, in 1868, both Chambers supported the formation of the Straits Settlements Association which became an influential body in London (of which more in Chapter 3).

The Chambers were interested in more than commerce; the Singapore mercantile community used the Chamber to speak for business interests to government on a variety of subjects. With Adam Logan as secretary from 1850 to 1869, the Singapore Chamber of Commerce was very active in politics. However, the Chamber fell into disarray and factionalism during this period, apparently through errors of political judgement and inept management, and in 1860 the Chinese withdrew from it. Notwithstanding the Chambers' occasional successful influence on government in economic matters, their political agitation was resented and they failed to become the basis of mercantile participation in Straits government.

Individually, however, leading merchants gained formal roles in government after the S.S. became a Crown Colony in 1867. William Henry Read, a partner in A.L. Johnston & Co., was the first non-official member of the new Legislative Council; others were Thomas Scott, a partner in Guthrie & Co., and Thomas Shelford, a partner in Paterson, Simons & Co. Read had a long history of opposition to Indian government and had been a leading campaigner for the transfer of the S.S. from the authority of India to that of the Colonial Office (Turnbull, 1969, pp. 28–29).

While the merchants sought a degree of local government and the extension of government services, they opposed strongly any attempt to raise local charges or introduce taxes. London, understandably, was unwilling to cut the Straits loose from India until reassured that local government revenue would be sufficient to cover local expenditure for civil and military purposes; in particular, the British government was worried about the potential cost of defending Singapore. Given Raffles' commitment to free trade, which had been extended to all the S.S. in 1826, and the limited scope for taxing land and agriculture in each settlement, there was no tax base which was directly related to commercial or productive activity in the Straits. The S.S. were administered at a loss, which fell on India, and the local authorities could not afford to concede any demands for the provision of further government services or infrastructure.

Consequently, it was to the pleasures and vices of the Asian communities, especially the Chinese, that the authorities turned for reliable sources of revenue. They adopted the system of tax farming, whereby the rights to levy consumer taxes on spirits, opium, and at times gambling, were sold, usually by public auction, to persons or groups known as tax farmers. These were invariably Chinese, except for the Indian toddy farmers (Turnbull, 1972, pp. 196–201; for a fuller treatment of the tax farm system as it continued into the 20th century, see Butcher, J. in Butcher and Dick, 1993). With the population growing and trade expanding, the tax farms provided a revenue base which moved in parallel with economic activity. However, the yield from the farms was still insufficient to fund the needs of the government; so in the 1850s the supreme government in India toyed with the idea of introducing income and stamp taxes in the Straits. These proposals aroused strong resistance. A move to introduce stamp duties in 1851 was abandoned in the face of merchant opposition; in 1860 public meetings in Singapore and Penang were held to petition the distant authorities against the introduction of income tax into the Straits. Local opposition was not confined to the European merchants and "the Chinese complained bitterly that they already paid a large part of the revenue through the opium and arrack taxes" (Turnbull, 1972, p. 202).

Governor Cavenagh proposed an imaginative scheme for a progressive local income tax but the idea did not proceed when the authorities in India resiled from the income tax proposal. In the end, government revenues were brought to the necessary level by the 1863 extension to the Straits of the India stamp tax. This was begrudged but accepted by the merchants, and it did not trouble the smaller businesses which did not use stamp-liable documents. The revenue of the S.S. was thus finally secured on bases of economic activity, and it is worth noting that the excise farms still provided two-thirds of the total (Turnbull, 1972, p. 204).

Chapter 2

Taking Root: 1850s–1870

Money

Banks entered the Straits Settlements (S.S.) in the 1840s, initially from British India. In earlier times, Guthries had represented the London bank Coutts, and Bousteads the Hong Kong and Shanghai Banking Corporation. The Union Bank of Calcutta was the first bank to open in Singapore, in November 1840 (Buckley, 1965, p. 351). It was followed in 1846 by the Oriental Bank Corporation and then by the Chartered Mercantile Bank of India, London and China (1855), the Chartered Bank of India, Australia and China (1859), the Asiatic Banking Corporation and the Commercial Bank of India in the 1860s. Up to 1902, at least 11 banks operated at various times in the S.S., usually beginning in Singapore or Penang before later extending into the peninsula. They represented, first, British, and later, Dutch, French and American interests. These early banks were "exchange banks" rather than deposit and loan institutions. They reduced the need for costly and risky international movements of specie and bullion by matching the foreign receipts with the foreign payments of Straits enterprises. Bank notes were first issued by the Oriental Bank in 1849, followed some years later by the Chartered Bank, the Chartered Mercantile and the Asiatic. Demand deposits, however, were never of much importance before the 1870s. In those times, the medium of local trade and commerce was coin (specie) but such currency was always scarce, and its insufficiency continued until near the end of the 19th century. Monetary habits ran ahead of legalities: silver dollars were current coin long before being given legal tender status, and early bank notes in use were not legal tender either.

The entry of banks after 1840 initially did little to alleviate the scarcity of currency because the banks concentrated on exchange transactions. They were slow to undertake note issues and to create demand deposits by making local loans and advances. So silver dollars remained the means of local trade. Silver dollars were popular because of their further and wide acceptability in regional trade, especially between India and China, which was so important to the infant S.S. The silver dollars were originally of Spanish origin — the Carolus dollar issued under Charles V of Spain, "its weight and fineness, being well known, appear to have made it a great favourite with the natives of the various islands" (Spalding, 1924, p. 108). This coin was known colloquially as the "pillar" dollar because it bore the device of the twin pillars of Hercules; however, the Malay world took the device to depict cannons and so the term "cannon" dollar also became current. After 1824, the dollar was minted in Mexico, hence the further term "Mexican" dollar, and for a period "it had the distinction of being the most widely circulated coin in the history of the world. It was circulating throughout the two American continents, in the West Indies, in the Pacific islands, and Japan, and in Asia from Siberia to the tip of Malaya" (King, 1957, p. 3). However, the provision of this dollar was problematic because it originated in Mexico, and "its supply could be checked, limited or stopped or its silver content debased without warning" (*ibid.*). The Indian authorities of the S.S. attempted to circumvent this problem by replacing the dollar with the silver Indian rupee, which was made legal tender for the S.S. in 1837. This move was unpopular in Singapore and resisted from the beginning by the mercantile community. At a meeting on 24 October 1837, the Chamber of Commerce resolved to protest to the Bengal authorities, declaring that "substituting Company's Rupees as the only legal currency of these Settlements, in place of Spanish dollars and Dutch guilders — the present currency — would be highly injurious to the commerce of the said settlements, besides entailing considerable expense on the Government" (Buckley, 1965, p. 318).

Despite further legal tender enactments over the next 20 years to entrench the rupee, the Straits population steadfastly resisted the use of the rupee. It was an inconvenient unit of account, it never became a circulating medium and it was entirely unsuitable for the China trade. Matters came to a head after the Legal Tender Act of 1855. The mercantile community in Singapore had been agitating against that Bill in 1854, after the Treasury in Singapore had been instructed to substitute the rupee for the dollar in their payments. The *Singapore Free Press* remarked that "it behoves the community of this place, as well as the two other Straits settlements, to lose no time in offering their determined opposition to the progress of these mischievous and most ill-judged measures" (Buckley, 1965, p. 595).

A public meeting in Singapore in 1854 resolved to petition the Legislative Council of India against enforcement of the rupee and suggested instead that a British (i.e., East India Co.) dollar be introduced (*ibid.*). The issue boiled on over the next few years, with the government keeping its accounts in rupees and the population conducting their transactions in dollars, until in 1857 the East India Co. retreated and ordered the resumption of the use of the dollar in S.S. government transactions and accounting. It was not until 1867, when the S.S. became a Crown Colony separate from the Indian government, that the rupee was entirely discontinued and legal tender status at last bestowed on the silver dollars "issued from Her Majesty's Mint at Hong Kong, the silver dollars of Spain, Mexico, Peru and Bolivia and any other silver dollar to be specified from time to time by the Governor in Council" (Chalmers, 1893, p. 386).

Put simply, the entry of banks meant that the stock of money in the Straits was no longer determined wholly by the balance of international receipts and payments, reflected in an inflow of specie when positive and an outflow when negative. Banks could add to the money supply by the issue of bank notes or the creation of demand deposits, so long as these bank obligations were fully convertible into specie on demand. The banks needed only to be sure of access to specie to redeem their obligations on demand. Therefore, local note issues were subject to stiff reserve requirements (see Drake, 1969, pp. 12, 106–107 for a fuller exposition of these matters).

Bank notes were first issued in the Straits in 1849 by the Oriental Bank, in denominations of $5 and $100 (Buckley, 1965, p. 506). In 1861 the Chartered Bank raised its status in Singapore from "agency" to "branch" in order to obtain the privilege of issuing bank notes and, for the same purpose, that Bank later opened branches in Penang and Malacca. The Chartered Mercantile and the Asiatic also issued notes in Singapore. With the rapid growth of trade in Singapore "the pressure on the available means of payment was heavy, and therefore the note issue was not only profitable to the bank itself but of convenience to the mercantile community at large" (Mackenzie, 1954, p. 105). However, public confidence in bank notes was not wholly secure, as was revealed in 1864–1865 when there were very heavy failures of both European and Chinese merchants; this led to "foolish panic among the natives about the security of bank notes, and there was a run upon the banks for silver in place of them (Buckley, 1965, p. 711).

As Mackenzie recounts:

> *The Chinese became convinced that the Chartered Bank and the Chartered Mercantile were both dangerously involved, and this condition was fortified by the refusal of the Chettiars to accept bank notes in payment for opium. The Indians demanded silver dollars, which resulted on Sunday the 7th May 1865 in bank notes changing hands in the bazaar at 3 or 4 per cent discount. Next morning, as soon as the banks opened, the Chinese poured in to exchange their notes for silver dollars and they were running around the counters until business ceased for the day after 3 pm, by which time the Chartered Bank had paid out nearly 80,000 dollars for its notes and the Chartered Mercantile rather less. Next day, the manager was standing by for a repetition of the run, but overnight the more substantial Chinese merchants managed to quieten the petty traders, most of whom had no bank accounts, and the run was checked. Nevertheless, some time passed before the Chartered Bank regained its former level of note circulation, partly because the Asiatic Banking Corporation seized the opportunity to start a note issue of its own.* (Mackenzie, 1954, pp. 105–106.)

The Asiatic had earlier lured away the local manager of the Chartered Bank, by the offer of a much larger salary, and he took with him much of the Chartered's local business. Competition among banks was very keen and the arrival of new competitors forced down interest rates and profit margins. The trade slump of 1864–1865 continued into 1866 and the financial crisis deepened. The Asiatic Bank and the Commercial Bank of India collapsed, and in July the Chartered was hard pressed. "The whole of the Bank's current deposits had been withdrawn and the note issue ran down from 250,000 dollars to 40,000" (Mackenzie, 1954, p. 107). The situation was slow to improve and businesses were cautious. The Chartered lost European customers but retained loyal Chinese. Only the Oriental Bank stood strong, doubtless buttressed by the fact that its customers included the largest importers of opium. Nevertheless, the Chinese and European firms indebted to the Chartered remained sound and by late 1867 large mercantile firms and Chettiars were again buying the Chartered's bills. The Chettiars, who financed most of the opium trade, were shrewd and dealt only with sound Chinese merchants. The Chartered thrived on its business with these two groups, and by 1872, a large share of its assets consisted of short bills discounted by those groups and longer term loans and advances to them.

In mid-1872, panic again arose in the bazaar. The Chartered saw it coming and reduced its commitments. Within a few months, the largest opium firm in Singapore failed, owing £40,000 to the Oriental and £125,000 to the Chartered Mercantile; but the Chartered escaped almost without loss. The Chartered continued to grow its business; its note circulation increased from $319,000 in 1872 to $874,000 in 1880, by which year it was the most popular bank in Singapore (Mackenzie, 1954, pp. 109–110).

Credit, Competition and Default

The slump of the 1860s gave rise increasingly to trade defaults. The recurrent problem is mentioned in regard to 1858, 1860, 1864 and 1867 by Turnbull (1969 and 1972) and intermittently in contemporary newspapers and in surviving correspondence of merchant firms.

Credit sales, and the inevitable proportion of defaults, continued because of the extremely keen mercantile competition that existed in the Straits ports. Any merchant who attempted to enforce hard terms of payment was quickly cut out by competitors who were prepared to offer easy credit to the Chinese and run the risks. As put by Turnbull, "the *Free Press* complained in 1867 that a Chinese immigrant had only to invest in a clean jacket and an English-made umbrella and any European merchant in Singapore would gladly open his door to him to grant him credit" (1972, p. 181).

The Chinese further exploited the extremely competitive situation in which the European merchants found themselves and refused to settle in cash for imports. Worse, from the merchant viewpoint, the Chinese middlemen began to insist that the merchants pay hard cash (sometimes even in advance!) for produce exports, at the same time as they themselves demanded extended credit for imports:

> *The merchant who can only sell his piece goods and other imports to the Chinese at three month's credit, is unable to get a picul of produce of any description without paying hard cash for it on delivery. Therefore, to a great extent, credit is merely the outcome of competition among the merchants themselves to obtain purchasers for their goods, and it is not at all surprising that they occasionally get hold of slippery customers. (Straits Times, 12 September 1885.)*

A meeting of the Chamber of Commerce in June 1864 decided to reduce the term of credit allowed to buyers of imports from three, to two, months and to encourage firms not in the Chamber to act similarly. Inevitably, however, the agreement was disregarded because of the force of competition among the European, especially German, firms and led ruinously to more and more extended credit, rather than the restraint which could have averted failures (Buckley, 1965, p. 712). Again, in 1872, Boustead & Co. proposed at a Chamber of Commerce meeting that all imports be sold at two instead of three months' credit but found few supporters.

Of course, defaults by Chinese middlemen threatened seriously the European merchant firms and brought some to bankruptcy. The most significant failure was that of the long-established house of D'Almeida & Sons in 1864, which failed with liabilities exceeding a million Straits dollars (Wong, 1960, pp. 165–166; Turnbull, 1977, p. 43). John Purvis & Son also ceased business with a deficit of over $500,000 (Bogaars, 1955, p. 99, n. 4). The constant pressure of competition led many merchants into overtrading and then to failure or absorption. Those who survived and prospered avoided overtrading and were good judges of the credit worthiness and reliability of local traders.

A further reason for the caution of Singapore's European merchants in giving credit to Asians was the fear that the goods would fall into the hands of pirates. Malay race seamen from various parts of the eastern archipelago (as far as Mindanao) prowled the eastern seas and the Malacca Straits, preying on small Asian craft carrying trade goods. Piracy waxed and occasionally waned from the 1820s to the 1870s and flourished in the 1850s and 1860s: in 1864 it was said that "only half the Asian craft from the archipelago succeeded in reaching Singapore" (Turnbull, 1972, p. 42; Gale, 1987, p. 45). Singapore had limited Admiralty jurisdiction, and therefore complained repeatedly to the Indian authorities in order to maintain naval protection. In the end, piracy declined in the 1870s largely because of a greater British naval presence in the eastern seas to support the China trade, together with the extension of Dutch power in Sumatra and British power in the Malay peninsula.

Merchant Investments in the Malay States, and Conflicts Therein

The merchants in the Straits ports had long been involved not only in trade but also in activities related to trade, such as bill-broking, moneylending, shipping and insurance agencies. The early middle years of the 19th century saw the merchants attempting to diversify from complete reliance on trade and to develop interests in the production of exportables. They made various investments in the cultivation of nutmeg, clove, gambier, sugar, coffee and gutta percha in Singapore and on the Malay peninsula. Alexander Guthrie, for example, had 2,000 nutmeg trees in Singapore in 1849 (Loh, 1958 and Turnbull, 1972, *passim*). Ker, Rawson & Co. engaged in Johore, in association with Temenggong Ibrahim (who was formerly involved in piracy!), to control the lucrative trade in gutta percha. When Ker returned to England, his partners reformed as Paterson, Simons & Co., continued to act as Ibrahim's agents and became the first firm to operate in Johore in search of peninsular trade and investment opportunities (Gale, 1987, p. 49; Turnbull, 1977, p. 52). In 1861, William Thomas Lewis, a former Resident Councillor and Commissioner of Police, obtained permission from the Sultan of Perak to establish a large-scale commercial rice farm near the Krian river. Unfortunately, the scheme encountered political difficulties and was abandoned (Gale, 1987, pp. 47–48). Merchants were attracted to these activities in part by the high prices prevailing for spices. However, Loh claims that after 1850 "the trend of reverting to trading pure and simple was discernable" and attributes this reversion more to the enhanced opportunities which were created by the advent in mid-century of steamships, telegraphy and the opening of the Suez canal, than to the natural and commercial hazards of tropical agriculture (Loh, 1958, pp. 21, 25). While these developments facilitated and encouraged greater international trade, the interest of the British merchants in the production of exportables did not diminish and they continued to probe the Malay peninsula for investment opportunities, often in alliances with Chinese and Malay associates.

Rich deposits of tin were discovered in the Larut district of the Malay state of Perak in 1848. This discovery encouraged the few Chinese miners who were already prospecting in the region and attracted new Chinese immigrants in large numbers. The Larut discoveries revealed resources of tin ore which were far beyond the extractive capacities of the Malay inhabitants. Therefore, the Malay rulers, in return for heavy taxes on tin production, invited Chinese entrepreneurs to import labour for mining. However, the Malay chieftans were unable to maintain order among rival factions of Chinese who fought over the occupancy of mining land and the monopoly of supplies to the miners. The British did not undertake tin mining on the peninsula at this stage but they were concerned for law and order behind the prosperous ports of the S.S. and were eager to engage in the development of the peninsula.

Guthries negotiated for tin mining concessions in Selangor in the 1860s and 1870s. These protracted negotiations required taking sides with one or other of two warring Chinese clans, the Kah Yeng Chews (Hokkien), who belonged to the Ghee Hin secret society, and the Fei Chews (Kheh/Hakka), who belonged to the Hai San secret society (Cowan, 1961, pp. 46–48 outlines the history of these societies). Parkinson puts the complexities of the Chinese factions concisely:

> *The miners came, in part, from the Five Districts immediately round Canton and in part from the Four Districts which lay further afield, although still in the Province of Kwang Tung. The hostility between the*

*Five and Four Districts had caused war in Kwang Tung in 1855–68 and
enmities remained among the Chinese immigrants. The See Kwans (Four
Districts) were Cantonese members of the Ghee Hi or Triad secret society. The Go Kwans (Five Districts), with Hakka or Kheh allies, formed
the Hai San or Tokong secret society.* (Parkinson, 1964, pp. 74–75.)

Guthries sided with the Fei Chews (Hai San society), whose tin mining
activities they had been assisting for five years by way of considerable
loans to Yap Ah Loy, the clan leader. Guthries also gave financial aid
and armaments to Tunku Kudin of Selangor who sided with the Fei
Chews in the hostilities. Also supporting the Fei Chews were Thomas
Scott, Dr Robert Little, Teo Siong Chwee, Hoo Ah Kay (Whampoa) and,
importantly, James Guthrie Davidson, the influential nephew of Guthrie's
London partner, James Guthrie, who was also on side.

In favour of the Kah Yeng Chews were William Henry Read of A.L.
Johnson & Co., Tan Kim Seng (leader of the Hokkiens in Singapore) and
the Rajah Mahdi of Selangor. Also sympathetic to that side were George
Lipscombe of Boustead & Co., Sir Peter Benson Maxwell (the Chief
Justice) and Thomas Braddell (the Attorney-General). Furthermore,
Braddell in his private practice, was legal adviser to the Sultan of Johore,
who was fearful of Fei Chew infiltration to his state.

Tunku Kudin, who relied on Fei Chew support, was a significant figure in Malay politics in the mid-19th century. (In earlier records and writ-
ings, Tunku Kudin is variously referred to as Tengku Kudin, Tunku dia
Oodin, Tunku Zaiuddin, Tunku Zia'u'd-din; in this work, for simplicity,
Tunku Kudin is preferred.) Kudin was a lesser prince of Kedah, who had
no appanage of his own. However, he had the good fortune to marry the
daughter of Sultan Abdul Samad of Selangor. As the old Sultan's son-in-
law, he was appointed *"wakil yam tuan"*, a term loosely translated as
"viceroy", and acknowledged as such by British officials. He prevailed
over rival princes, gaining control of the Kelang/Klang region and some
authority throughout Selangor, but he never acceded to the Sultanate and
eventually retired to Kedah (Andaya and Andaya, 1982, pp. 147–151;
Cowan, 1961, pp. 71–77).

James Guthrie Davidson became Tunku Kudin's legal adviser and in
1873, Kudin rewarded his backers with a concession of substantial tin

mining rights in Selangor on generous terms. The opposing parties disputed this grant on the grounds that Tunku Kudin was not yet the Sultan of Selangor but merely Viceroy. However, Guthries moved speedily to counter that argument and to have the concession transferred to their newly formed Selangor Tin Mining Co. (see Cunyngham-Brown, 1971, *passim*, on which all this section draws, especially pp. 152–153; see also Gale, 1987, pp. 56–57, which describes the Penang riots of 1867 and claims that rival secret societies of Hokkiens and Cantonese were responsible not only for the riots but also for the conflicts over the tin mines in Perak).

It is evident that there were serious divisions between two separate groups of Singapore businessmen and officials, the alignment of each group with opposing Chinese factions and contending Malay factions, and at a time when local hostilities on the peninsula were fierce, especially in the tin-rich states of Selangor and Perak. All this was bringing the British government, concerned for the wealth and safety of Singapore, closer to intervention in the Malay states which occurred in 1874. Before then, however, a large step forward was the 1867 transfer of power over the S.S. from the India Office to the British Crown directly. To this key development we now turn.

Governance Developments in the Straits Settlements

As described in Chapter 1, the Singapore merchants had long chafed under rule from India, whether by the East India Co. initially or, following its abolition, from 1858 by the India Office. In 1857 the merchants sent a petition to the British parliament. This petition first of all supported the demands of the European merchants in Calcutta for the abolition of the East India Co.; secondly, it asked that the S.S. be separated from India and ruled directly from London. The petition claimed that Calcutta treated the S.S. as part of British India and disregarded local concerns, notably lack of representation in government, inadequate judicial systems, failure to prevent piracy, weakness in dealing with the Chinese and using Singapore as a dump for convicts (Turnbull, 1977, p. 71). Although the petition failed to gain the support of most Penang merchants, the House of Commons received it favourably. London, however, did not go the whole way. The East India Co. was abolished and, by Proclamation of 1 September 1858,

Her Majesty took up direct government of all her Indian dominions, but London jibbed at separating the S.S. from the India Office.

India was glad to give up the Settlements but unwilling to spend time unravelling the Straits' complicated accounts to the British Treasury's satisfaction. The Colonial Office complained in 1860, "The India Office seem in the same breath to admit a deficit and claim a surplus". The enthusiasm of those who clamoured for change also harmed the cause of transfer since, Read, Crawfurd, other former Straits residents in London, and the Singapore chamber of commerce, all produced optimistic but conflicting financial estimates, which served only to increase suspicion in the Treasury and the Colonial Office. (Turnbull, 1977, p. 72.)

The British Treasury broke off negotiations. London lacked proof that the S.S. would be self-supporting. Nor would the Colonial Office agree with the merchant view that Singapore was of vital strategic importance to the British Empire.

In the end, the extension of the Indian Stamp Act to the S.S. in 1863 — initially opposed fiercely by the merchants — brought the Straits' finances into balance. Also in 1863, the British government asked the Governor of Hong Kong, Sir Hercules Robinson who was on his way back to his post after home leave, to stop at Singapore and report about the Straits. He favoured transfer of authority to the Colonial Office. Events then stalled again because the British government refused to finance military expenditure in Singapore. However, in 1866, the War Office desired to establish a military base in Singapore as an alternative to Hong Kong where support for a base was declining because of health and social problems. So, on 1 April 1867 the S.S. became a Crown Colony and administration from the India Office ceased (See Turnbull, 1977, pp. 72–75 and Buckley, 1965, pp. 754–780).

In Singapore, the immediate consequences of the "Transfer" were minimal. There was largely disinterest at the change among the Asians and disappointment among the Europeans. Much of the previous mercantile dissatisfaction had already been addressed and eased by the assiduous and wise rule of Colonel Orfeur Cavanagh, the final Governor appointed by the India Office. He had presided over the solving or diminution of the problems of taxation, currency, piracy and convicts and, in a burst of impressive public works, including many fine buildings which are treasured in modern times. Cavenagh was respected and much liked locally but he departed peremptorily, and most unhappily, when displaced from office and never officially advised of the Colonial Office's choice of his successor (Turnbull, 1977, pp. 72–80). Notwithstanding their affection for Cavenagh, the merchants had hoped for more vigorous progress in the aftermath. The new Governor arrived in Singapore on 16 March 1867; of him more anon.

Despite mercantile disappointment in its early consequences, the Transfer had a most powerful effect in the longer term: by providing a large degree of local governance and executive authority, it opened the door for the promotion of political change and economic development in the Malay states. As we shall see, the first Governor appointed by the Colonial Office was a contentious figure in the S.S. colony, and showed not publicly his intentions about the Malay states. In 1874 his successor interpreted liberally a Colonial Office request to investigate the situation in the western Malay states and concluded the landmark Pangkor Engagement with the Chiefs of Perak. This action quickly provided indirect British rule, in the name of the Malay Sultans, of the western Malay states and led swiftly to British participation in Malay governance and rapid economic development of the rich natural resources of the Malay states.

Chapter 3

Straits Politics and Trade Infrastructure, 1867–1873

Before continuing the story of British intervention, encroachment and investment in the Malay States, it is necessary to pay some regard to the very significant, mid-19th century, international developments in technology, communication and markets. These things all increased greatly the attractiveness to Britain of embracing the Malay peninsula within the British commercial empire. It is first important to consider the to and fro of local politics and governance, which eventually played out in a way that allowed for active British authority in the western Malay states.

Straits Politics

The first colonial Governor, Colonel Harry St George Ord, arrived in Singapore on 16 March 1867. He came from the governorship of Bermuda with high hopes and zeal. However, despite over six years of overdue administrative reforms, material progress and general prosperity under his rule, he was greatly disliked by the merchants and hostile towards them (Turnbull, 1977, pp. 80–82; Buckley, 1965, pp. 785–789; Cunyngham-Brown, 1971, pp. 111–118). A similar situation prevailed also in Hong Kong, where colonial governors Sir John Davis (1844–1848) and Sir John Pope Hennessy (1877–1882) were both hated by the mercantile class (Criswell, 1981, pp. 88–92). It is worth noting that the Colonial Office instructed these governors, as with Ord, to make the colony self-supporting, improve the administration, strengthen law and order and look to the welfare of the resident Chinese, who comprised the predominant population in the Straits Settlements (S.S.).

The mercantile and professional men agitated against Ord in Singapore and also in London, through the Straits Settlements Association (SSA) which was formed on 31 January 1868 in London, with branches in Singapore and Penang. Its first President was John Crawfurd, who had been Resident of Singapore 1823–1826 and was a contemporary of Stamford Raffles. Other founders included William Napier, James Guthrie, Ellis James Gilman and Dr Robert Little. Paul Tidman, of the Borneo Co., was Secretary of the Association until his death in 1889. The founders "viewed with some uneasiness" the apparent extravagance of Governor Ord, especially in relation to the size and cost of the new Government House. Over the years of its existence (until 1920 when it was subsumed into the new Association of British Malaya), the SSA

> ... *interested itself in nearly every matter concerning the public life and growth of the Colony, such as the constitution of the Legislative Council, the defences of Singapore and military contribution, questions dealing with currency, prisons, railway construction, land tenure and the Crown Lands Act, the annual estimates and legislation including the Municipal Ordinance, the Burials Bill, the Societies Bill, and other important matters too numerous to mention here.* (The Secretary, British Malaya, May 1926, p. 31.)

Many merchants, professionals and officials served the SSA. They were men who "were largely responsible for the successful development of the Colony, and did not neglect the interests of the place after leaving it" (*ibid.*).

Governor Ord got off to a bad start. His seemingly aloof behaviour at the ceremony of inauguration of the Colony and installation of its Governor drew much criticism from the entrenched old guard:

> *Then, under another salute, stalked in Governor Ord, without removing his hat, and sat down on a chair on the dais without taking any notice of any one. The impression thus created was never removed and was justified in the years that he remained in the Straits.* (Buckley, 1965, p. 787.)

Mutual dislike arose almost immediately between Ord and Sir Peter Benson Maxwell, Recorder of Singapore under the authority of the India Office and shortly to become Chief Justice of the S.S. Colony. The cause of friction was the Governor's pretention to a degree of honour beyond that bestowed legitimately on his office. As Governor, Ord desired to be styled "His Excellency" and regarded as the sovereign's representative. Although it had long been customary within Britain's crown colonies for Governors to be addressed as "Excellency", this was by common consent and courtesy rather than by mandate of right. The Colonial Office addressed governors by name only, and in the Privy Council it had been judged that a colonial governor did not represent the sovereign generally but only in respect of the specific functions delegated to him by the terms of his commission.

Ord was probably unwise to insist on his interpretations of precedence because his stance evoked confrontation and continued lack of co-operation from Maxwell, ironic because Ord became a Knight in the Order of the Bath on assuming his office and Maxwell was made Chief Justice and a member of Ord's government.

While Orfeur Cavenagh, the last India Office governor, was "found to have been greatly beloved (at least on the eve of his departure) and Ord was considered, by contrast, to be tyrannical, overbearing, quarrelsome, and tactless … it will be more helpful to look at the Colony from the Governor's point of view." (Parkinson, 1964, p. 4.) There is little doubt that the small ruling community of the S.S., comprising officials, professionals and the mercantile class, was a comfortable oligarchy well set in its views and customs which were far from the formalities and practices which Ord had experienced in other crown colonies. The situation has been summed up nicely:

> *Ord provoked considerable ill-feeling in reorganizing the administration, in clearing up carelessness and corruption and demanding higher standards of efficiency. His attack upon nepotism and abuses of patronage, which had been accepted as normal practice before 1867, raised a fury of resentment. In his attempt to make the judiciary conform to normal colonial practice, Ord found himself in head on collision with the Chief Justice, Sir Benson Maxwell, who as Recorder of Singapore had enjoyed personal independence and considerable rights of patronage under the Indian regime. Maxwell marshalled the non-official*

> *members of the legislative council [mostly merchants] to support him in*
> *open conflict with the Governor, but the Colonial Office insisted on*
> *bringing the Straits judiciary into line with all other crown colonies, by*
> *making the Chief Justice responsible to the Governor in Council.*
> (Turnbull, 1977, p. 81.)

Maxwell must have been rankled by Ord's pretensions and jealous of his precedence; under the India Office Maxwell, as Recorder, had enjoyed being arbiter on points of procedure and representation of the Crown (Parkinson, 1964, p. 10).

The lax administration in Singapore under India Office authority extended to the casual, albeit friendly, personal style of Governor Cavenagh, who took no pains to maintain the status of his position. Cavenagh lived in a modest house, Leonie Hill, in Grange Road, well out of town. There he conducted much of his official business, to the inconvenience of officials and the community who worked in town. Sure enough, Governor Ord thought that a central and imposing Government House was needed urgently.

When cut loose from India, the revenue of the S.S. was just sufficient to cover its then expenditures. Ord was given strict instructions by the Secretary of State, Lord Carnarvon, not to propose any new items of expenditure "without conclusive proof that the funds necessary to cover such charges will be forthcoming when required". The financial position was lean and problems were looming (Parkinson, 1964, pp. 22–23). Also, Ord was concerned by the fact that nearly all government revenue came from impositions on "the pleasures and vices" of the generally poor Asian population, whereas the Europeans paid trivial taxes despite their vast incomes. Accordingly, Ord rashly told the Legislative Council at the end of 1867 that future circumstances might necessitate the imposition of direct taxation, including perhaps import duties. However, even the merest hint of taxes on trade was enough to arouse ferocious protest. In April 1868, the SSA protested to the Colonial Office about Ord's remarks (C.O. 273, 28 April 1868).

The Secretary of State, now the Duke of Buckingham and Chandos, had already read the speech, which Ord had included in the Singapore Government Gazette of 27 December 1867, and had written the following reproof to Ord: "I observe that in that speech you refer to the possible imposition of Import Duties. I regret that you should have used any language which was calculated to raise the impression that so vital a change would be authorised."

Again, in July 1868, after receiving the SSA protest, he wrote:

> *With regard to your insertion in an official document of a reference to Import Duties, I think it was unfortunate. The language used was not unlikely to be interpreted as a threat…. I give you credit for your desire to secure an equitable apportionment of taxation between Europeans and Natives…, but you cannot be unaware of the extreme sensitiveness of Commerce. You cannot be unaware of the very prevalent opinion that the prosperity of Singapore is based on its character of a free port — an opinion which, whether right or wrong, is widely held and by high authorities — it is certainly held most tenaciously by those who are most interested in the prosperity of the Straits Settlements.* (Parkinson, 1964, pp. 24–25.)

Tempers flared again in April 1869 when the SSA sent to the Colonial Office a memorandum deploring the first two years of colonial administration and highly critical of the Governor. The Colonial Office forwarded this memorandum to Governor Ord. "This led to angry exchanges with the Governor, and to the organization of public protest meetings in Singapore under the chairmanship of Read, the senior non-official in the legislative council" (Turnbull, 1977, p. 82).

The Singapore opponents of Ord made repeated accusations of administrative waste and personal extravagance, most notably in the matter of the new Government House. However, as noted above, there was no Singapore residence, fitting for the dignity of a Governor, provided when Ord arrived. So it was most reasonable that a suitable Government House be built to provide both a residence for the Governor and offices for his administration. However, there was much local resistance to the idea for fear of increased taxes to pay for it and in envy of the symbolic dignity which the old guard begrudged the Governor. Moreover, the ambitious design of the house would be expensive to construct and supplements were also required. The *Straits Times* had a picnic on the proposal with frequent criticisms, such as "Its cost however will do full justice to its size". Stung by this, Ord informed the Colonial Office that the *Straits Times* contained "unfounded and foolish statements made by the Editor in the full knowledge of their incorrectness" (Parkinson, 1964, p. 27, n. 2). Similar public criticisms were made of the Governor's decision to replace the unseaworthy government vessels with a new steamship, a cutter and a new engine for the launch. However, as later events in the Malay States proved, it was necessary for the government to have a fast ship at the ready for maintaining speedy communication and personal presence with Penang, Malacca and the ports of the western Malay States.

After a couple of years of uneasy truce, Governor Ord's final year in Singapore, 1873, was marked again with contention from the mercantile class.

To start with, Ord sought to stem abuses surrounding the immigration of Chinese coolies, who flooded into the Straits ports in order to find work in the Malay States and the Dutch East Indies. Some idea of the volume of immigration can be gleaned from marine office returns available for 1865–1866; their statistics show a total of 17,439 persons, of whom 14,279 landed in Singapore, 3,008 in Penang and 152 in Malacca. Of the Singapore arrivals, 7,418 transhipped to the other S.S., the Malay States and Mauritius. Interestingly, there were only 655 females among the Singapore arrivals (*Straits Settlements Annual Report*, 1865–1866, p. 44). The so-called "coolie trade" was run by Chinese secret societies but the labourers were treated disgracefully. The early immigrants from China were free and unassisted, but immigration was commercialised as the mining boom grew. Intending migrants who could not afford the fare from China to Malaya were offered passages on credit or indenture contracts. On arrival in Malaya, the indentured labourer was claimed by the employer to whom he was bound by the terms and conditions of his contract. "Credit passage" immigrants were detained on ship until the recruiter found employers for them. The labourers had a bad time: the recruitment system was little better than livestock trade and the Chinese referred to it as "the pig business". Ill-treatment of the migrants continued in mining work and attendant evils, such as the truck system of payment and the provision of opium on credit, cemented the labourer's bondage to the contractor or employer. However, enlightened Chinese leaders petitioned the government to control and superintend Chinese immigration rather than curtail it. Ord attempted to do this by means of the Chinese Coolie Immigration Bill, which he introduced in September 1873, shortly before his departure from the Straits on 2 November.

> *This modest bill proposed merely to register immigrants, not to enforce contracts nor provide reception depots, but it provoked a fury of opposition from European merchants, legislative councillors and the English-language press, in defence of the treasured principle of free immigration, which was held to be the life blood of the Straits economy.* (Turnbull, 1972, p. 83.)

At the same time, Ord introduced a bill to reform judicial procedures which, *inter alia*, sought to abolish the Grand Jury, reconstitute the Supreme Court, enlarge the judiciary and create a court of appeal. The mercantile community was again outraged. The European merchants convened a public meeting on 15 September where it was alleged that the abolition of the Grand Jury would remove "the last check between arbitrary government and justice to the people". The European non-officials then resigned from the Legislative Council (Whampoa, the Chinese member, remained). Nevertheless, the Criminal Procedure Bill was passed in their absence and approved by the Colonial Office.

Governor Ord saw William Henry Read, of A.L. Johnston & Co., as the instigator of these rebellious actions but he dutifully sent to the Colonial Office a report of the protest meeting and the resignation of the non-official councillors. The merchants had also sounded off about the Chinese immigration bill, the letting of revenue farms and the abolition of municipalities. In writing to the Colonial Office on 1 October, Ord made his defence:

> *The mercantile community which constitutes the society of this place takes hardly any interest in anything beyond their own immediate business. Most of them openly avow that they came here solely to make money and in some of the most important firms it is made a stipulation that its Singapore Members take no part in public affairs. It is not therefore to be wondered at that upon political and even social questions not immediately and apparently affecting their own interests, they are seldom found to have formed any fixed convictions.* (Parkinson, 1964, p. 104.)

The Secretary of State for the Colonies now inclined to Ord's view of things. He rejected a further plea from the merchants that the non-officials be reinstated to the council and that ordinances should not be put into effect until approved by the Colonial Office "since he objected to the principle that the non-official minority should exert even a temporary veto on legislation" (Turnbull, 1972, p. 84).

Although Sir Harry Ord departed from his post generally unloved in Singapore, he was able to report, on the eve of his departure, evidence of substantial material progress in the Straits during his term of office. Singapore's trade increased over 50% in the period of his rule, the government revenue and expenditure account was in balance and Ord left the colony with its credit balance at over £240,000.

Finally, Ord deserves recognition and some credit for his efforts to advance Britain's movement into the Malay States. From the start of his tenure, Sir Harry travelled energetically around the Malay States and even into Siam (Cowan, 1961, pp. 54–60; Sadka, 1968, p. 40). Ord was privately sympathetic towards British advancement into the Malay States and in this he was at one with his otherwise mercantile critics. But London's policy — inherited from the India Office — forbade British interference in the Malay States. In 1868 the Secretary of State instructed Ord accordingly,

> *The policy of Her Majesty's government in the Malayan peninsula is not one of intervention in native affairs.... If merchants or others penetrate disturbed and semi-barbarous independent states ... they must not anticipate that the British government will intervene to enforce their contracts.* (Turnbull, 1972, p. 84.)

A prime example of this hands-off policy occurred in that same year when Paterson Simons & Co. complained to the Colonial Office about the seizure of their property by the Raja Bendahara of Pahang and the refusal of H.M. Government to intervene (C.O. 273, 1868, Misc. 4768, 6605, 7723).

Nevertheless, while on leave in England in 1871–1872, Sir Harry made personal contact with the Secretary of State (now Lord Kimberley) and pressed for a more active policy; but the Colonial Office refused to budge and Ord was tied to its policy of non-intervention. Deterred from positive forward action, Ord did whatever he could to help responsible steps ahead. For instance, in 1872 he encouraged the Bendahara of Pahang to assist Tunku Kudin to regain control of the Klang and Selangor rivers. Peace on the peninsula was essential to the growth of trade and in tacitly supporting Kudin the Straits governor "stepped beyond London's policy of non-intervention" (Andaya and Andaya, 1982, p. 148).

From late 1872, Governor Ord reported frequently to the Colonial Office about disturbances in the Malay States. He forwarded various requests for intervention from European and Chinese merchants and also a specific proposal from the Acting Lieutenant Governor of Penang for the annexation of Perak, or at least the appointment of British residents (Sadka, 1968, p. 45).

A later Governor, Sir Frank Swettenham, who had served as a junior under Sir Harry Ord felt that Ord, in comparison with his predecessors, was an exception in visiting the Malay States in the early years of his rule but that intermittent calls were too infrequent to lead to anything more than polite acquaintance. However, "in justice to Sir Harry Ord it should be said that, in the later years of his rule, he had made efforts to exert his influence in the Western states by sending a senior member of the Straits Government to make enquiries, and by personal visits of his own" (Swettenham, 1942, p. 27).

In October 1872, the Singapore Chamber of Commerce complained to Governor Ord that British subjects were not encouraged to do business in the Malay States nor were their interests protected. Ord replied, "If persons knowing the risks they run owing to the disturbed state of these countries, choose to hazard their lives and properties for the sake of the large profits which accompany successful trading, they must not expect the British Government to be answerable if their speculation proves unsuccessful". Ord enclosed all this correspondence with a long despatch to the Secretary of State in which he described in detail the unsettled conditions in the western Malay States and the steps he had taken to bring about a better situation. Lord Kimberley wrote back, "In reply to your despatch no. 189 of 6th November last I have to express to you my approval of the answer returned by you to the Chamber of Commerce of Singapore on the subject of a letter addressed to the Chairman of the

Chamber by certain traders of Malacca who are interested in trade with Selangor" (Swettenham, 1942, pp. 27–28).

Let Sir Frank Swettenham have the last word on the first Colonial Governor: "Sir Harry Ord was a big and very masterful Governor, of great ability and strong character. He was not at all popular; the Press found fault with him in almost every issue…. But Sir Harry, who came to Singapore … to find his charge with a budget that would not balance, left the Colony in 1873 with a respectable sum to its credit" (Swettenham, 1942, pp. 16–17).

One hundred and forty years later, Singapore displays little recognition or memorial to Ord's governorship. There is merely Ord Bridge, which bears no commendation of its namesake and is the most modest of the many quays along, and spans over, the Singapore river bearing the names of past governors.

External Influences on Straits Trade

Two related developments drove trade growth and infrastructure building in the S.S. during the years immediately after the transfer of authority from the India Office to the Colonial Office. These developments, both of external origin, were the conversion of international shipping from sail to steam power and the opening of the Suez Canal in 1869. Soon afterwards, a further boost resulted from British political intervention in the Malay States from 1874.

Steamships from Europe had been calling in Singapore and Penang since 1845 but the early steamships were expensive to run, owing to heavy fuel consumption; the consequent need for coaling stops resulted in slow voyages. However, improvements in the design and performance of marine engines in the 1860s quickly made steam competitive with sail. World steam tonnage exceeded three millions by 1870, nearly double that of 1860, while the aggregate tonnage of sailing ships was dropping. Nevertheless, sailing ships still dominated the freight trade between Europe and the Far East up to 1870. The opening of the Suez Canal in 1869 changed the situation dramatically. The fastest sailing passage from London to Singapore around the Cape of Good Hope was 116 days in 1867, whereas in 1870 the steamship "Shantung" made the voyage from Glasgow to Singapore through the Canal in 42 days, stopping at Port Said,

Suez and Penang. Sailing clippers could not effectively use the Canal because they were apt to become becalmed there and in the Red Sea. "No tea clippers were built after 1870 and within five years of the opening of the Suez Canal the pick of the tea trade had passed to specially designed steamers" (Bogaars, 1955, p. 104). Through the Canal, the reduction in the time that goods were in transit was estimated at 10 weeks on average. "In effect, the changeover from sail via the Cape to steam via Suez more than doubled the earning capacity of a Singapore merchant's capital" (*ibid.*, p. 106).

For passengers, mail and small items of freight, the steamer eliminated the delays and expense of transhipment, with disastrous economic costs for the hospitality, services and wharf industries in the intermediate ports. A steamer could earn more in 12 months than a sailing vessel of similar capacity because it could make at least two round trip voyages in that time compared with the single annual voyage of most sailing vessels. "Singapore became an essential link in the chain of British ports and coaling stations, which stretched from Gibraltar, through Malta, Suez, Aden, Trincomalee and on to Hong Kong or Australia" (Turnbull, 1977, p. 86).

In 1870, Singapore's exports and imports rose sharply and healthy trade continued throughout the 1870s. "Between 1870 and 1879 the value of the year's imports increased from 39 to 56¼ million [silver] dollars, and of the exports from 31½ to over 49 million dollars" (Bogaars, 1955, p. 101). The trade resurgence soon added to mercantile competition, including from Dutch, French, Swiss and, especially, German merchants. Prior to 1860, only three German firms were established in Singapore: Behn, Meyer & Co. (1840), Rautenberg, Schmidt & Co. (1849) and Zapp, Bauer & Co. (1854). But despite quiet trade in the 1860s, 15 new German firms entered in the latter part of that decade, especially subsequent to the opening of the Suez Canal, and five more were established in the 1870s. In 1875, the *Brisbane Courier* stated,

> *The Germans are pushing their way irrepressibly in the East.... It is said that they manage to sell their goods much cheaper than their British competitors, or will accept lower salaries, as the case may be. But it is also fair to state that their success is in a great measure due to the thorough Commercial education they have received.* (Bogaars, 1955, p. 111.)

While British men were studying the classics, their German rivals were learning modern languages and commerce (*ibid.*). The Germans were said to have done about one quarter of Singapore's foreign trade in 1865 (Wong, 1960, p. 168). The Germans were also very active and prominent in Penang, where they were major traders and civic leaders (Khoo, 2006, gives an excellent account of the German community in Penang).

All told, the opening of the Suez Canal and the coincident development of steamships ushered in a period of expansion of East–West trade. Singapore waxed prosperous on its superb location, Britain's naval supremacy and the general growth of world trade. The entry of more mercantile firms, shipping companies and banks, and the 1870 extension of telegraphic contact with Europe via India, solidified Singapore's position as the hub of East–West trade. The laying of the telegraph cable from Penang to Singapore was a substantial technical task for the Straits Settlement authorities (Anson, 1920, pp. 294–295).

Singapore Infrastructure

The port facilities of Singapore lagged behind trade. To start with, as Parkinson, a naval historian and Singapore professor, perceptively noted:

> *The original town of Singapore had been built in the wrong place; wrong that is to say in relation to the eventual position of the harbour. The river mouth around which the first settlement clustered had come to nothing except as a landing place for native craft. The new harbour, where the depth was sufficient for large ships, was remote from the business centre with its offices and godowns.* (Parkinson, 1964, pp. 9–10.)

The Singapore River served essentially as the town's first port. Ships anchored in the Roads facing the shore, as near as possible to the mouth of the river. Lighters carried merchandise from there to the merchants' godowns lining the river bank at Boat Quay and took Straits produce on the reverse journey (Tate, 1989, p. 6). Boat Quay, so named by 1823, was on the western side of the river, and there Alexander Guthrie obtained from the government a 999-year lease of 27,922 square feet of sandy bog and clay on which to build a godown (Cunyngham-Brown, 1971, p. 44). However, the P. & O. Steam Navigation Co. built a wharf on New Harbour in the 1850s and a number of merchant firms followed suit.

The first slip and graving dock was built in the same period, by Captain William Claughton, on the north side of New Harbour, to the west of the P. & O. wharf (Cunyngham-Brown, 1971, pp. 144–147). In the 1860s, The New Harbour Dock Co. and the Tanjong Pagar Dock Co. were developed, respectively, by the mercantile rivals Paterson Simons & Co. and Guthrie & Co. (the latter in association with Tan Kim Ching). In New Harbour, by 1869, there were three graving docks, one slip, and wharves belonging to P. & O., Jardine Matheson & Co., the Borneo Co. and the Tanjong Pagar Dock Co. However, the trade recession of the mid-1860s meant that there was, for a time, surplus capacity, with insufficient work for even one dock. Business improved after the opening of the Suez Canal and a revival of world trade. Also, liberalisation of trade policies in the Dutch East Indies, and in Siam under King Chulalongkorn, brought regional trade through Singapore. Increased traffic saved the Tanjong Pagar Dock Co. and underpinned its expansion, to the extent that by the end of the century it had absorbed all but one of its competitors in docking and wharfage. Tanjong Pagar Dock Co. paid its first dividend in 1872, opened the Victoria Dock in 1868 and the Albert Dock in 1879, by when it employed some 1,700 men and had added wharfs and coal stores to its facilities. The number of vessels visiting the Tanjong Pagar complex rose from 99 steamers and 65 sailing ships in the half-year end to August 1869, to 185 steamers and 63 sailing ships during the corresponding period in 1872. In the full year of 1879, 541 steamers and 91 sailing ships used the Tanjong Pagar facilities (Bogaars, 1955, p. 128).

The distance of about one and a half miles from the Singapore wharves at New Harbour to the town centre had lacked any good land connection, and so the growth of shipping trade provided a spur for improved roads between the port and the town, where the merchants' godowns and offices were located. Three new roads — Anson Road, Keppel Road and Coral Street — were constructed in the late 1870s, which served the need. Plans were made also for the construction of railways and tramways to make the link but these works did not proceed immediately; attempts to fulfil them gave rise to disagreements among the business classes and, again, conflict between merchants and the Governor.

Construction of a railway line between city and port was a contentious matter. The idea commanded general commercial and official support as the easiest way to link the north-western wharves, the Tanjong Pagar complex to the southeast and the town centre further east. A railway was universally desired but who would pay for it? As early as 1865, plans were drawn up for a rail line to run from near the Patent Slip and Graving Dock Co. (Claughton's dock) to the fish market at Teluk Ayer, near Raffles Place. The government agreed to this on the basis that the companies would contribute the capital and the line would be completed in three years. However, the trade slump thereafter caused companies to demur and nothing was done then. In 1871 when trade had revived, the Tanjong Pagar Dock Co. sought government permission to build a short line between their premises and the town centre; other companies wanted the longer line originally proposed and that was favoured by government. The Colonial Office agreed in December 1871, provided that the line was built either by the Straits government or by a private company which would represent the interests of the public. The latter was not forthcoming and Governor Ord advised the Colonial Office that there was no prospect of a private company making the railway. That left open the possibility of the government undertaking the work.

Apparently for fear of the budgetary burden of government investment in the railway (with implications of taxation), protests were made to the Colonial Office by the SSA in London and by Bousteads and other merchants in Singapore. Ker & Co. added that the Tanjong Pagar Dock Co. was also in opposition to construction of the longer line by the government. On the other hand, the P. & O. Steam Navigation Co., whose wharves were located near the western extremity of the proposed line wrote to the Colonial Office in September 1872 saying that "a line of railway is in reality becoming indispensable" in view of the growth of trade and expansion of the port. However, nothing came of the railway plan. In the 1880s, tram lines were laid connecting the Tanjong Pagar docks to Collyer Quay in the town but, unfortunately, the tramway service was not profitable and ceased in 1894 (Bogaars, 1955, pp. 129–135).

Monetary and Financial Matters

Reference has been made already, in Chapter 2, to the sustained resistance in the S.S. to attempts by the imperial authorities in India to impose the rupee currency upon the S.S. In 1867 the new Crown Colony administration of the S.S. moved swiftly to discontinue the legal tender privilege of the rupee and in its stead bestow legal tender status on the silver dollars issued variously in Hong Kong, Spain, Mexico, Peru and Bolivia.

However, there remained a shortage of currency in the Straits because provision of silver dollars was beyond the control of the Straits government; it was instead dependent on an inflow of silver dollars through a surplus in the balance of international trade and investment. The emergence of bank money in the S.S. from 1850 gave some, but not complete, alleviation to the chronic shortage of currency, which persisted until the end of the century when an official Straits dollar was introduced (of which more anon).

As recounted above and at the end of Chapter 2, the taxable capacity in the S.S. was severely constrained so long as it was forbidden to impose taxes on trade, the largest source of Straits income. Therefore, there was limited scope for government to undertake public works. Table 6 — expressed in rupees — shows that government revenues and expenditures for the last seven years of India Office rule (it should be noted that disbursements do not include the annual charge levied by India for military support of some 750,000 rupees, equivalent to about £50,000 at the exchange rate of 1s 4d for one rupee). Table 7 — expressed in pounds sterling — shows the pattern of government revenues and expenditures in 1863–1864. The deficit of £4,096 was attributed to the unusually high levy for military support in that year. The Stamp Tax introduced in 1863 was enough to more than balance the budget of local revenue and expenses but not to cover also the military levy in full. It is evident that prior to the introduction of the Stamp Tax the S.S. did well to provide public works from its revenues; in Singapore, these included

Table 6.   Straits Settlements, Treasury and Municipal Receipts and
Disbursements, 1859–1860 to 1866–1867.

Year	Treasury (Indian Rupees)	Municipal (Indian Rupees, '000)
	Receipts	
1859–60	1,254,531	355
1860–61	1,532,842	378
1861–62	1,614,836	408
1862–63	1,713,305	408
1863–64	1,956,758	414
1864–65	1,972,593	443
1865–66	1,965,965	438
1866–67 (est.)	1,931,725	
	Disbursements	
1859–60		442
1860–61	1,226,300	350
1861–62	1,228,072	400
1862–63	1,231,890	439
1863–64	1,206,326	392
1864–65	1,176,669	387
1865–66	1,234,418	431
1866–67 (est.)	1,266,309	

Source: Report on the Progress of the Straits Settlements from 1859–1860 to 1866–1867, Singapore, Government Printer, 1867.

improvements at New Harbour, two bridges over the Singapore river, and the construction of roads between Singapore town and Ayer Rajah and between Tanglin and New Harbour (S.S. Annual Report, 1862/63, p. 21).

The Municipality of Singapore was accounted separately from general revenues and expenditures. In 1858/59 the municipality was in financial difficulty, despite increased receipts, because of large expenditure on sanitary works, with indifference to financing capacity (S.S. Annual Report, 1858/59, p. 73). In most years, however, the municipal receipts

Table 7. Straits Settlements, Revenue and Expenditure, 1 May 1863–30 April 1864.

REVENUE	£
Excise and other farms	137,521
Land and forests	6,705
Stamp tax	26,175
Law and Justice	9,957
Public works	4,222
Marine	4,300
Miscellaneous	3,029
TOTAL	191,909
EXPENDITURE	£
Collection of revenue	7,585
Allowances under treaties	6,279
Public works	27,350
Salaries and expenses of departments	25,861
Law and Justice	22,564
Marine	14,908
Retired allowances and grants in charity	5,402
Education	2,239
Miscellaneous	2,744
Military	114,932 81,073
TOTAL	196,005
Deficit	4,096

Source: Cameron, 1965, pp. 209, 232.

(from assessments on houses and carriages, and fines from the magistrate's court totalling £25,207 in 1863/64) were more than adequate to provide for the police, the maintenance of public roads and bridges, etc., totalling £22,963 in that year (Cameron, 1965, pp. 209, 231–233).

It is not surprising that mercantile interests resisted, strenuously and stridently, government attempts to undertake infrastructure investment and major public works. The spectre of taxes on trade was ever present. After the slump of the late 1860s, the trade of the S.S. boomed again. In the period of Ord's rule, export values leapt from $26.7 million in 1868 to $41.7 million in 1873 and import values from $31.6 million to $47.9 million in the same years (Bogaars, 1955, p. 140). No wonder the merchants were uneasy!

Chapter 4

Opening the Peninsula, 1874–1896

The disorder in the mining regions of Perak, Selangor and Negri Sembilan, described in Chapter 2, continued and showed signs of escalation as the numbers of immigrant Chinese labourers kept growing. At the same time, Malay authority was very weak because of ongoing conflicts about succession to the Sultanate of Perak among several claimants and their various Chinese and European supporters. Sir Harry Ord had been cultivating the ground for the establishment of some sort of British authority but he did not move fast enough for the would-be merchant investors in the Straits Settlements (S.S.) and London, whose investment in tin mines (along with Chinese) was already considerable (Andaya and Andaya, 1982, p. 145), and it was also substantial in gambier and pepper plantations in Johore (Cowan, 1961, p. 37).

Ord's successor as Governor, Sir Andrew Clarke, arrived in Singapore on 4 November 1873 with Colonial Office instructions to investigate and report on the state of affairs in the west coast Malay States but his swift actions went well beyond "investigate and report". Clarke was of the "act first and explain later" school. He convened a gathering of Malay chiefs on Pangkor island, at which Raja Abdullah was declared to be Sultan of Perak, to be supported by a British resident adviser. Although it was far from fully accepted by the Malay factions, the "Pangkor Engagement" held fast and a British government presence was implanted on the peninsula. The background, conduct, outcome and consequences of this signal event on Pangkor have been fully recounted and discussed in official records and many substantial historical studies, among which the works by Parkinson (1964), Cowan (1961), Sadka (1968) and Gullick (1992) are excellent. Special mention should also be made of Swettenham (1942). Frank Swettenham, then a junior official (and years later, Governor) in the S.S. was "the man on the ground" at the Pangkor meeting and his first-hand account of the event must be regarded as authoritative. Another excellent account of the circumstances of the Pangkor event, and subsequently, is an original approach which sets these developments in the worldwide context of British colonialism at large (McIntyre, 1967). In this context, the author deals with personalities and attitudes within the British governments of Gladstone and Disraeli, especially the several Secretaries of State for the Colonies and Colonial Office officials showing, among other things, repercussions of events in other colonies upon attitudes to the Malayan issue. McIntyre also illustrates the ambitions, personal views and breadth of experience of governors Ord and Clarke in their various colonial roles before coming to Malaya. Each wanted to restore, consolidate or burnish his reputation, perhaps with an eye to further promotion.

***

It was in January 1874 that Governor Clarke obtained "the key of the door" for British intervention in the Malay States. On 13 December 1873, Governor Clarke gave a dinner in Government House. After dinner, he asked one guest, the ubiquitous William Henry Read, to stay behind for a talk. In this conversation, Read asked the Governor if he intended to take any action in the unfortunate situation in Perak. In Read's words, "He said: 'I am ready at a moment's notice if I can get the key of the door.' I said, 'Give me a fortnight and I will get it for you.' I immediately drew up, and had translated into Malay, a letter [for signature by Abdullah and other chiefs]" (Parkinson, p. 121). The letter was duly prepared, dated 30 December, and returned to the Governor, with the desired signatures, on 9 January 1874. The crucial part of this letter reads,

> *We and our great men wish to make a new treaty of lasting friendship with the English Government, which will benefit both sides, and we,*

together with our great men, to show our good faith, ask of our friend,
Sir Andrew Clarke, for a man of sufficient abilities to live with us in
Perak ... and show us a good system of government for our dominions,
so that our country may be opened up and bring profit, and increase the
revenues as well as peace and justice.... (Parkinson, p. 122.)

It may be noted that this version of Abdullah's letter varies from the original draft, prepared for Abdullah by Read, wherein Abdullah and the chiefs ask for a Resident to "assist and advise them to carry out the Government of the Country in such a way as to develop its resources, secure the administration of justice and the peace and happiness of the people". The final version, signed only by Abdullah, merely asks for "a man" to "show us a good system of government" (Cowan, p. 183, n. 22). Be that as it may, the outcome of the Pangkor meeting was the establishment of Raja Abdullah as Sultan of Perak and him undertaking to accept a British Resident "whose advice must be asked and acted upon on all questions other than those touching Malay Religion and Custom" (Parkinson, 1964, p. 137).

Although this "key of the door" account is widely accepted as the Malay appeal for British intervention and protection, it needs to be acknowledged that Raja Abdullah had "in 1873, asked Governor Ord to send him a British officer 'to teach him how to rule the country', a request which was reported to Clarke as soon as he assumed duty" (Swettenham, 1942, p. 30). Governor Clarke, of course, was under instructions from the Secretary of State for the Colonies, Lord Kimberley, by a letter given dated 20 September 1873, the day of his departure from England, Ord still being Governor in Singapore. The long letter of instruction was accompanied by a memorandum on past relations with the Malay States. The key paragraph of the letter reads:

I have to request that you will carefully ascertain, as far as you are able,
the actual condition of affairs in each state, and that you will report to
me whether there are, in your opinion, any steps which can properly be
taken by the Colonial Government to promote the restoration of peace
and order, and to secure protection to trade and commerce with the
native territories. I would wish you especially to consider whether it
would be advisable to appoint a British officer to reside in any of the

States. Such an appointment could, of course, only be made with the full consent of the Native Government, and the expenses connected with it would have to be defrayed by the Government of the Straits Settlements. (Parkinson, 1964, p. 112; Swettenham, 1942, p. 31.)

Notwithstanding the many references to the protection of trade and commerce and the creation of further opportunities for investment in the Malay States, there was a more fundamental reason for driving British policy towards intervention, namely the fear of another European power encroaching on the Malay Peninsula. It has been argued by some historians that this fear was played upon and translated into a forward policy by the activities of one Seymour Clarke, a man of good repute in the City of London, well-connected to Singapore as the brother-in-law of W.H. Read, and venture associate of James Guthrie Davidson whose syndicate held tin-mining concessions from various Malay chiefs. Seymour Clarke (not related to the incoming governor, it seems) spoke with Sir Robert Herbert, Permanent Under-Secretary in the Colonial Office, and then wrote to him on 18 July 1873 saying that he had recently heard from "an old resident of Singapore" who was close with Malay chiefs [undoubtedly, W.H. Read] and "From his channels of information this 'old resident' thought it likely that the smaller states of the Peninsula would put themselves under the protectorate of some European Power, and failing England he had heard Germany mentioned as the most likely" (Cowan, 1961, p. 167). Drawing on related stirrings by the promoters of a tin-mining venture in Selangor and also the "Viceroy" of Selangor [Tunku Kudin], Cowan argues that Seymour Clarke's letter was an ultimatum — if Britain did not act, local interests would invite another power to do so. Sir Robert Herbert saw it that way too. He suggested to the Secretary of State [Lord Kimberley] that Britain should consolidate her position in the Peninsula without taking on any major risks or responsibilities (Cowan, 1961, p. 165).

Kimberley agreed and wrote the following Minute:

It would be impossible for us to consent to any European Power assuming the Protectorate of any State in the Malayan Peninsula. I think we might send this to the F.O. and enquire whether they would see any objection to Sir A. Clarke being instructed to endeavour to extend the

Treaties with Salangore and the other Malay States by a stipulation that they should not enter into any treaty ceding territory to a Foreign Power or giving such Power any rights or privileges not accorded to us. (Cowan, 1961, p. 168.)

Cowan concludes from this that it is clear from the terms and timing of this Minute that Seymour Clarke's letter instilled a palpable fear of European rivalry and precipitated the abandonment of the policy of rigid non-interference.

In essence, at the gathering at Pangkor, the assembled chiefs, with varying degrees of enthusiasm, all accepted Raja Abdullah as Sultan of Perak. By Article VI of the Engagement entered into by the Chiefs of Perak at Pulo Pangkor dated 20 January 1874, the Sultan was to "receive and provide a suitable residence for a British Officer to be called Resident, who shall be accredited to his Court, and whose advice must be asked and acted upon on all questions other than those touching Malay Religion and Custom". Article X provided "that the collection and control of all Revenues and the general administration of the Country be regulated under the advice of these Residents" (Parkinson, 1964, p. 137).

The Aftermath of Pangkor

Governor Clarke had rushed the Engagement. A contemporary critic, Sir Peter Benson Maxwell, the former Chief Justice, wrote "honestly, the treaty could mean no more than that the Sultan would give serious attention to the advice offered" and that the Malays who "imagined they were treating for a guide, had accepted a master and signed their country away to foreign rule" (Gullick, 1992, p. 15). Parkinson concludes that "the Malay chiefs were hustled (as Malays can usually be hustled) into apparent agreement" (Parkinson, 1964, p. 139).

In consequence, there followed, until 1878, years of confusion and conflict. Clarke's precipitate policy went disastrously wrong. Back in England, Sir Harry Ord told the Colonial Office that Clarke's lack of "an intimate acquaintance with Malay character" had led him to suppose that "they accepted what in fact they simply did not understand" (Gullick, 1992, p. 14). Clarke is on record for a disparaging view of Malays when he wrote to the Secretary of State that "the Malays, like every other rude Eastern nation, require to be treated much more like children, and to be taught; and this is especially in all matters of improvement, whether in the question of good government and organization, or of material improvement" (Sadka, 1968, p. 53).

A most telling critique of Clarke's impetuosity was made by Colonel Archibald Anson, Lieutenant-Governor — based in Penang — of the S.S. 1867–1882, who wrote,

> *There can be little doubt that these chiefs did not fully realise what they were asked to agree to; or if they did, had no intention of acting up to it. One of them ... came to me a few days after the affair at Pankor, and said he was so confused and upset at that meeting, that he did not rightly know what the Governor wanted him to do.*

Anson added in a later passage, "Of course, on the occasion of the engagement at Pankor, when the chiefs were all on board the Government steamer, with a man-of-war close by, they appeared to agree to everything that was proposed to them" (Parkinson, 1964, pp. 137–140). It is easy to believe that the chiefs were truly confused. As Sir Harry Ord wrote, generously, in 1876,

> *It was natural that Sir A. Clarke, seeing the readiness with which his terms were agreed to by the natives, should have taken it for granted that they understood what was required of them, and were really prepared to accept our assistance in governing their country according to our views. But a more intimate acquaintance with Malay character would have prevented this misconception.* (Parkinson, 1964, p 140.)

The Pangkor Engagement was unworkable in its stated terms "because there was no meeting of minds, Malay and British, as to what in practice the new system was to be" (Gullick, 1992, p. 15). At least until 1878, there was no unambiguous understanding or official definition of the Residential system, despite much confusing and at times acrimonious correspondence between London and Singapore. "In the course of time all concerned were obliged to face the fact that the Pangkor formula, i.e. offering advice to the Ruler was a 'fiction'" (Gullick, 1992, pp. 16–17).

Governor Sir William Jervois (1875–1877) who succeeded Clarke had no time for mere advice and attempted to grasp the nettle by proposing a scheme for direct administration of Perak by Queen's Commissioners, together with an advisory body of Malay chiefs. This idea, and continuing strife in Perak, led in 1876 to a

> *celebrated recrimination between Carnarvon [Secretary of State for the Colonies] and Jervois over what had gone wrong, the former decided that the experimental Residential system based on the Pangkor formula should continue, adding that 'I am, however, disposed to approve your proposal of establishing a Council of mixed Malay chiefs and British officers'* (Gullick, 1992, p. 39. The recriminatory correspondence can be found in Parkinson as Appendices C and D, pp. 327–370; see also Parkinson, 1964, pp. 310–316).

Yet the Colonial Office continued for some time to insist that in form, at least, the fiction must be observed and Governor Sir William Robinson in 1878 stipulated that "the Residents have been placed in the Native States as advisers, not rulers, and if they take upon themselves to disregard this principle they will most assuredly be held responsible if trouble springs out of their neglect of it" (Gullick, 1992, p. 17).

Meanwhile, Governor Clarke had moved, characteristically quickly, to implement the terms of the Pangkor Engagement. Captain T.C. Speedy was appointed immediately as Assistant Resident in the Larut district. The heads of the rival Chinese factions signed an undertaking to disarm and not again break the peace. On 20 January 1874, a Commission, consisting of three British officials — F.A. Swettenham, W.A. Pickering and Colonel Dunlop — and the heads of both Chinese factions, was established to ensure that the undertakings were enforced and to rescue captive Chinese women and children, who had mostly been abducted from Penang. The Commission realised that restoration of peace and order depended fundamentally on settling the disputes over mining territory. No one possessed any documentary proof of title to mining land. The Mantri of Larut had given no more than permissions to fell the original jungle, while he imposed taxes on tin extracted from the cleared ground after it had been smelted ready for export. The Commission drew a line across the mining area and proposed allocating the land on one side to the Five Tribes faction of Chinese and on the other to the Four Tribes. The factions agreed and peace reigned thereafter (Swettenham, 1942, p. 35).

Selangor quickly followed Perak, thanks largely to the blandishments of young Frank Swettenham, who had been sent by Governor Clarke to live with old Sultan Abdul Samat at Langkat. On 1 October 1874, the Sultan signed a letter of request for a Resident (Cowan, 1961, pp. 206–207).

Residents were selected, but for bureaucratic reasons it was not until November that their appointments were formally gazetted. They were: James Wheeler Woodford Birch as Resident of Perak, with T.C. Speedy as Assistant; J.G. Davidson as Resident of Selangor (a contentious appointment in view of his commercial intimacy with the Malay Viceroy, Tunku Kudin, to whom Davidson was "allocated", while F.A. Swettenham was appointed to continue to advise the Sultan as Assistant Resident at Langkat); Captain Tatham as Assistant Resident of Sungei Ujong (Cowan, 1961, p. 210; Parkinson, 1964, pp. 184–185). By implication from the Pangkor Engagement, the British authority granted in Perak was thus extended, seemingly without demur, to the other two states where Chinese feuds threatened British interests (Cowan, 1961, pp. 215–217).

Apart from mining, there was little external investment in the Malay Peninsula. The exception was Johore, where by 1864 there was more than $1 million invested by Singapore Chinese in gambier and pepper plantations. The Temenggong (ruler) grew rich by controlling and taxing these agricultural developments (Cowan, 1961, pp. 36–39). Johore was essentially part of the Singapore economy. It was separated by only a narrow channel of sea and its Malay ruler was on good terms with the Singapore authorities. Johore's development had been done mostly by wealthy Chinese in Singapore and its population was predominantly Chinese.

***

Increased world demand for tin from about 1870 caused its price to rise and production to increase. This led in 1873 to the formation of two companies to undertake large-scale mining on the peninsula. The Sungei Ujong Tin Mining Co. was a Singapore venture under the control of the local Dato Klana with its directors including two powerful men from

Singapore, Whampoa and R.C. Woods. Whampoa (Hoo Ah Kay) was the leading Chinese on the island; Woods was a solicitor in partnership with J.G. Davidson, himself the moving spirit behind the Selangor Tin Mining Co.

That company was to have a working capital of at least £100,000 and was granted the exclusive right to mine all tin deposits in unworked areas of Selangor, Bernam and the Klang river region. The grant was for 10 years with the option of a further 99-year lease of land taken up. Also included were rights to appropriate further land which was not private property, to build roads and railways, to import workmen and build houses and shops for them. Moreover, in consideration of paying the Sultan 5% of gross mine production and $3 per bahar [= 400 lbs. approx.] on tin exported the company was spared all taxes and land-rents (Cowan, 1961, p. 142). The company was thus potentially all-powerful in Selangor, and so an important card in the hand of Seymour Clarke when pressing the British government to intervene in the Malay States.

The rapid expansion of tin mining needed not only capital but also much additional labour. A large full-time labour force was required to work the new-found tin deposits in Perak and Selangor. The shortage of labour was the problem of the Chinese entrepreneurs who, from about 1820, had been importing Chinese labourers. When the tin mining industry expanded after 1850, the flow of immigration increased. British intervention did not deter immigration and the Protectorate was content to let private enterprise solve its own problems. From the Chinese point of view, the combination of an efficient, honest and *laissez faire* British administration, with a resource-wealthy but sparsely populated land, constituted a positive attraction to industry and trade. At the same time, over-population, economic decline and rebellion in China (south and central China especially) encouraged thousands of Chinese to set out for the new world of Nanyang. It has been estimated that five million Chinese entered Malaya in the 19th century and a further 12 million between 1900 and 1940 (Ooi, 1963, p. 113). Most returned home eventually but enough stayed and procreated to result in four million Chinese residents by 1960. The early immigrants from China were free and unassisted, but immigration was commercialised as the mining boom grew. Intending migrants who could not afford the fare from China to Malaya were offered passages on credit or indenture contracts. On arrival in Malaya, the indentured labourer was claimed by the employer to whom he was bound by the term and conditions of his contract. Credit passage immigrants were detained on ship until the recruiter found employers for them. The labourers had a bad time — the recruitment system was little better than livestock trade and the Chinese referred to it as "the pig business". However, as we shall see, Governor Jervois took action to protect the immigrants.

***

To summarise, the British intervention in Malaya was seeded in Governor Ord's time and came to fruition under Governor Clarke. It was the result of a number of influences which came together in the 1870s. These were: a surge in the share of S.S. trade conducted with Southeast Asia and the consequent increasing attraction of exploiting the rich natural resources of the peninsula; a rise in the price of tin; increased concessions obtained and growing debts acquired in the Malay States by Singapore interests; civil disturbances and insecurity in the peninsula, which also threatened trade. These developments "created a bond of financial interest between European and Chinese circles in the Straits Settlements on the one hand, and the participants in the struggles in the Malay States on the other" (Cowan, 1961, p. 269). Succession problems and a lack of clear Malay authority made it opportune for the unauthorised intervention of Governor Clarke. The colonial authorities in London accepted that action without too much trouble, and to some extent relief, doubtless due to Whitehall's underlying fear that some other European power might gain a foothold in Malaya and threaten the free conduct of Britain's rich India–China trade.

***

For a few years after 1874, the governance of the three Malay States under the "advice" of British Residents was unsettled because of tension and acrimony between London and Singapore, between the S.S. government and the Sultans in Malaya, and among the rival Malay factions. Cowan (1961) and Parkinson (1964) deal at length with these several frictions which, in each case, were worked out over a few years. Notable illustrations of all this were the Malay murder of Resident Birch, consequent reprisals by the British, and the so-called Perak War. In that conflict, the Colonial Engineer, Captain R.E. Innes, was killed. Around the same time, restlessness in Sungei Ujong led to conflict which was resolved by the exercise of British force (Anson, 1920, pp. 329–343; Cowan, 1961, pp. 232–237; Parkinson, 1964, Chs. X–XI). However, all had mostly settled down by the end of 1878 and Britain controlled the destiny of all the protected states under the constitutional fiction of governance by "advice".

So settled were the tensions on the Malay Peninsula that, between 1877 and 1895, the residential system was extended to the other small states of Negri Sembilan (in addition to Sungei Ujong) and to Pahang. In 1896 a Federation of Protected Malay States (F.M.S.) was formed, made up of Perak, Selangor, Negri Sembilan and Pahang. The F.M.S. (described in more detail at the end of this chapter) gave Britain sufficient semblance of unified local governance to deal with, rather than the hitherto individual sovereignty of each Malay State. In 1885 Johore made a treaty with Britain by which Britain promised protection from external attack and would control the state's foreign relations. The Sultan of Johore (Abu Bakar) undertook not to interfere in other states and not to grant concessions to foreign (i.e. non-British) powers or companies. The traditional close and good relations between Johore and Singapore continued, although Johore did not join the Federation and not until 1914 did it accept a British Adviser. The political development of the Malay States between 1875 and 1914 has been comprehensively covered by Cowan (1961, Chs. 6–7) and needs no further reference here.

By the last quarter of the 19th century, the door of Malaya was formally open to British and Chinese investment and development.

***

Before the development of steamships and the opening of the Suez Canal linked the markets of Europe to Southeast Asia, the forest and sea produce of the Malay Peninsula was too small to attract much external capital investment. Nevertheless, British economic interests had been involved to some extent in production and finance in the Malay States well before 1874. Brief reference has been made above to mining and plantation activities. The scale of these was relatively small before 1874 but the

British investors had established connections and influence with the Malay aristocracy, and kept on good terms with Chinese entrepreneurs who were also probing the peninsula. Gradually, the Straits merchants became more deeply involved in peninsula affairs in order to protect their positions and, along with their Chinese associates, capture the development potential of the peninsula, which had been revealed by imperial expansion and the rapid growth of trade between Europe and Asia, in which Singapore enjoyed a unique position and great importance.

The 1874 Pangkor Engagement was the turning point in Britain's relations with the Malay states. From that moment it was inevitable that British rule would sooner or later encompass the whole peninsula as well as the S.S. However, this was to be a gradual process, as described earlier. Moreover, British enterprise advanced only slowly and the Chinese dominance of tin mining and commercial agriculture continued until the end of the century.

The first British Residents had to tread carefully. Malays simply did not see any distinction between "general administration" and "religion and custom" because the latter were fundamental in Malay society and underpinned their politics and actions. So it was impossible simply to transfer "administration" to British officials. The Residents also had large practical challenges. First, efforts to impose taxes to raise the revenue needed for state administration flew in the face of customary levies by district chiefs and led to resentment and resistance. Second, "slavery" — morally unacceptable in British eyes — was a traditional form of power which yielded significant economic resources to the Malay rulers. "In Perak slaves and debt bondsmen numbered an estimated 3,000 in a total Malay population of perhaps 50,000 (approximately 6 per cent)" (Andaya and Andaya, 1982, p. 160). These touchy matters called for wise, sensitive administrators with a deep understanding of Malay society and culture:

The difficulty in finding men sufficiently fluent in Malay to take up the new postings is a sobering comment on the lack of British interaction with Malays since the founding of Singapore in 1819. However, the newly created Straits Civil Service had established language requirements and one of its products, Frank Swettenham, spoke good Malay. (ibid., p. 161.)

Swettenham endeared himself to the Malay rulers but some other Residents did not. The unfortunate J.W.W. Birch paid with his life for the hostility which he aroused among the Malay chiefs in Perak.

The murder of Birch led to severe punitive actions by the new Governor of the S.S., Sir William Jervois. Sultans Abdullah and Ismail, and other chiefs, were sent into exile and their positions left unfilled for years. Raja Yusuf was appointed Regent of Perak by the British and installed as Sultan in 1887 (*ibid.*, p. 163). Swettenham commented that these firm actions "did more, in six months, to bring order and good government to Malaya, than could have been achieved by 20 years of peaceful persuasion" (Cunyngham-Brown, 1971, p. 159).

***

With more settled governance in the Malay States, the British merchants increased their speculations in mining and plantation agriculture, often in association with Chinese and other local connections. Sometimes the Chinese were the dominant financial partners; for example, J.A. Russell & Co. speculated in plantation development using funds lent by wealthy Chinese friends. Singapore merchants, both Chinese and British, were anxious to find profitable avenues for capital investment, which would complement their trading activities and offset losses. "The only really potentially rewarding areas for investment, able to service both the China trade and the growing markets of Europe, were commercial agriculture and tin mining" (Andaya and Andaya, 1982, p. 135). They were sniffing around for opportunities in these fields particularly. By the 1880s, it was apparent that the Malay States were becoming more important economically than the S.S. It is notable especially that by then Malacca had declined to complete commercial insignificance for the British. The census of 1881 recorded the resident European population of Malacca as 23 males and 9 females; there was no resident British merchant, nor was there any banker, newspaper or hotel (Bird, 1883, pp. 100, 112). By contrast, Malacca remained important to Chinese agriculture and commerce for a few more years. Malacca was the commercial hub of the tapioca industry. The wealthy Chinese of Malacca financed and controlled the tapioca industry in Malacca and neighbouring Negri Sembilan and

Chinese labourers were imported mostly from Hainan. Often aided by government grants, the Chinese built networks of cart-roads to connect tapioca plantations, factories and sources of firewood. The tapioca industry flourished from about 1860 until the early 1880s when tapioca prices fell drastically: planters suffered large losses, tapioca cultivation shrunk and labourers left the area (Jackson, 1968, pp. 56–58, 72–75). In the face of these difficulties and to combat wasteful shifting cultivation, the Straits government in Malacca then restricted the industry by denying new land leases.

Guthrie & Co. had commercial connections with the Malay States for many years before 1874, buying produce and selling imports, chiefly through Chinese intermediaries. The firm had also made loans to larger up-country businessmen including Sheik Abdul Rahman and P.M.S.P.K. Karrupan Chetty in Seremban and Tunku Kudin in Selangor. Yap Ah Loy of Kuala Lumpur, long associated with Guthries, enjoyed a $10,000 advance at 15% interest around 1874. When Swettenham, as Assistant Resident in Selangor, offered government loans at 10% to Chinese tin miners, Yap switched to this source of finance and sent only enough tin to Guthries to cover his interest rate (Cunyngham-Brown, 1971, pp. 156–157). These apparently high rates of interest were not unreasonable in the time and place when capital funds were scarce.

A coffee planter from Ceylon, Thomas Heslop Hill, arrived in Singapore in 1877 needing finance to plant coffee on the island of Pulau Ubin, in the Johore Strait. Guthries gave him an advance. However, the coffee venture failed there. Hill then undertook various road construction works in Selangor, Sungei Ujong and Perak, for which he was recompensed by land grants in those states, on which he planted coffee and prospered from 1886 to 1897. Guthries were the agents for these plantations. When then the bottom fell out of the coffee market, Hill sold the "Kamuning" estate in Perak, on which he had inter-planted rubber trees with the coffee. The buyers were the Guthries partners, Anderson and Scott, jointly with Loke Yew, the Kuala Lumpur millionaire (*ibid.*, pp. 161–164). The Guthrie's men thus became landholders on the peninsula and their firm took on the agency of the estate.

Guthrie & Co. records reveal many other joint speculations: in land for mining and/or plantation agriculture with T.H. Hill and Sheik Abdul

Rahman in Seremban in the 1890s; in the Bundi Tin Mining Syndicate in Trengganu with Chia Ah Cham and one (Sir) Catchick Paul Chater. The various partners in speculations on the peninsula were men of affairs in the S.S., both European and Asian and, not too conspicuously, officials as well as non-officials. Although it was generally frowned upon, business ventures by British officials were generally not illegal provided that the official kept his business activities out of the state in which he was currently serving (Drabble and Drake, 1981, p. 305). The internal resources of the merchant firms were limited in these times and could be depleted whenever a partner retired and withdrew his capital. Hence the firms utilised credit from banks, suppliers of imports and wealthy local Chinese (Drabble, 2000, p. 43).

The Baba Chinese from Penang and Malacca had long been associated with tin mining, supplying finance and Chinese labourers to the Malay chieftains who controlled the mining. In the 1830s, Chinese merchants from Malacca lent large amounts to the royalty of Selangor to finance mining in the Klang Valley. Unfortunately, the venture did not succeed and Sultan Mohamed was left with a debt of $169,000. However, success attended a later venture by Rajas Juma'at and Abdullah who in 1854 borrowed $30,000 from Malacca Chinese to open mines in the area that was to become Kuala Lumpur (Gullick, 1983, pp. 8–9). The Baba Chinese, who had become wealthy from trade, tax farms and property, were able to provide loans from their own resources and through their access to credit from the European merchant firms. In time, Chinese investors avoided the Malay chiefs and financed and managed Chinese miners directly, which weakened Malay authority. These elements were part of the complexity of the rivalries and strife on the peninsula which led to the British intervention in Perak. W.H. Read, who was so active in promoting that intervention, had a Chinese business partner, Tan Kim Cheng. Read and Tan had in 1866 been granted tax farms in Kelang by its Raja Abdullah in return for 20% of the profits. Soon afterwards, Raja Mahdi, son of a former ruler of Kelang gained control of the district and refused to pay the taxes. This led to the intervention of Tunku Kudin, son-in-law of the Sultan of Selangor. Raja Mahdi had finance from Chinese merchants in Malacca and Tunku Kudin was bankrolled by Singapore interests, including the Read–Tan syndicate and James Guthrie Davidson.

These alliances showed that both British and Chinese merchants were seeking economic footholds in the peninsula states. The Singapore authorities backed Kudin and by 1873 the Kelang and Selangor rivers were both under his control. Tunku Kudin then influenced Selangor to grant concessions over undeveloped mining areas to the Selangor Tin Mining Co., in which both Read and Davidson were involved.

***

Britain's role in the economic development of peninsular Malaya was greatly assisted by the establishment of the S.S. Civil Service. From 1867, recruits for service in the Straits were gathered by the Colonial Office in London, first by Colonial Office nomination but from 1882 by public competition. Similar civil services were established in each of the Protected Malay States and these were united in 1896 as the Malayan Civil Service, consequent on the formation of the F.M.S.

On arrival in the S.S. or a Malay state, cadet recruits were instructed in the Malay language, and by the 1880s, those who dealt with Chinese matters were sent to China to learn relevant dialects. Appointees normally served their whole career in British Malaya and so were able to develop connexions and understandings with Malay, Chinese and Indian communities which ran deeper than those of transient Governors (Turnbull, 1977, p. 85).

The British Resident in a Malay State was supported by a State Council, a legislative body containing the ruler, assorted aristocrats and chiefs, Chinese representatives and the Resident himself. Although advice to the ruling Sultan was tendered by the Council, the Resident dominated the Council and effectively determined the course of action. Beneath the Resident were District Officers, key officials who looked after the district revenues and finances, land rents, law and order, justice, public works, public health and the activities of the Malay ruling classes (Andaya and Andaya, 1982, pp. 172–174). In these ways the British officials ran the Protected States under the cloak of indirect rule. The Resident *par excellence* was generally thought to be Hugh Low "a consummate tactician" who administered Perak in 1877–1889 with great patience and sensitivity to Malay concerns, based on his deep understanding of their culture and language (Gullick, 1992, pp. 40–48, *passim*).

***

British economic interests spread from the central west states of Perak, Selangor and Negri Sembilan to Johore in the south and Pahang in the east. This "forward movement" was guided and driven by the energetic Frank Swettenham, who firmly believed that expansion was of benefit to the Malays as well as to British interests, political and commercial. The movement was helped along by Governor Frederick A. Weld (1880–1887) who took a keen interest in the Malay States which he visited frequently. Weld was much admired by Swettenham who wrote that:

> *He was greatly interested in all he saw, and made a point of meeting the Rulers and their Chiefs and talking to them about the affairs of their country and people. During his term of office, the great benefit he conferred upon the Malay States was the support he gave to the British Residents in their efforts to develop the country.... He supported any project designed to improve the lot of the people, especially the Malays, and he encouraged schemes for getting at the resources of the country.... The British Residents ... were convinced from the first that the resources of the States were so valuable that it was only necessary to get at them, and transport them to a market, to secure from reasonable duties far more than the cost of exploitation; and the Governor ... encouraged their efforts when a man with narrower views might easily have thwarted them.* (Swettenham, 1942, p. 80.)

In particular, Weld wanted to capture the wealth of Pahang, where Bendahara Ahmad had been selling many concessions to Singapore interests without any legal safeguard to control transference of concessions, such that some fell into the hands of London interests and were sold without regard for the territorial rights of Pahang chiefs or the fact that some areas were already being worked by local Malays or Chinese. In 1887, Weld sent his nephew, Hugh Clifford, as Britain's first "agent"; Clifford found the restricted role of agent frustrating, because he could not control the granting of concessions or prohibit the practices of slavery (Andaya and Andaya, 1982, pp. 166–168). Ahmad would not at first accept a Resident but, under duress, he finally gave in and in 1888 asked for one. The first Resident was John Rodger but he was disliked by commercial interests in Singapore and was not considered sufficiently firm in authority or administration. In 1896 Clifford was made Resident and served in that role for three years (Gullick, 1992, p. 364; Thio, 1968, pp. 93–94).

Rodger's failure to suppress a rebellious series of civil unrest and fighting, known as the "Pahang War", caused some uneasiness about the wisdom of the extension of British control into Pahang but the episode was brief and the British "forward movement" continued and its focus shifted to Johore (Andaya and Andaya, 1982, pp. 169–171).

Accompanying the forward movement was a strengthening of the position of the Chinese in the economy and as settlers. Chinese immigration via the S.S. was increasing, principally but not entirely to provide workers for the tin mines in the Malay States. It rose from 34,000 in 1878 to 103,000 in 1888 via Singapore alone. In 1890 the Chinese indirectly provided an estimated 89% of the revenue of Selangor, and they constituted about half the population of Perak, Selangor and Sungei Ujong when the first official census was conducted in 1891. Moreover, the Chinese dominated the emerging towns and cities: they were 79% of the population of Kuala Lumpur at that date (Andaya and Andaya, 1982, p. 176). However, no such Chinese dominance then existed in Pahang, which therefore suffered economic limitations (Heussler, 1981, pp. 94–96).

Governor Jervois, concerned about the neglect of Chinese welfare, appointed a commission of enquiry which recommended both firmer control of the Chinese and official protection of new immigrants. This led to the establishment of a Chinese Protectorate, with William Pickering as its first head. Pickering and his Protectorate were very effective for the better and his authority was extended to general oversight of the Chinese community in Singapore. Such oversight included Chinese prostitution, necessary when in Singapore alone 90% of the population were male. Prostitution was therefore tolerated and the Protectorate did not prevent the immigration of willing female prostitutes; but it did endeavour to stop forced prostitution and in 1881 it took over the administration of the 1870 Contagious Diseases Ordinance. The Protectorate also dealt with secret societies, with Pickering becoming a joint Registrar of Societies (which included other forms such as benevolent societies). Secret societies were thus recognised and registered in the S.S. but remained banned in the Protected Malay States. However, under strong leadership from Governor Cecil Clementi Smith, the secret societies were eventually suppressed under a Societies Ordinance from 1890 with the support of the then Protector, Pickering having retired in 1888 (Turnbull, 1977, pp. 86–90).

From about 1890 the Indian population of the Protected Malay States also began to rise rapidly through immigration, mostly of Tamil labourers from South India and Ceylon. This was in response to the labour needs of government and plantations. The large subject of Indian immigration will be dealt with in a later chapter, in connection with the development of the rubber industry. Suffice it now to say that by the 1890s, the British administration had connived at Chinese and Indian immigration which grew into permanent settlement in Malay lands and created distinct, enduring ethnic segmentation which persists in modern Malaysia. "The plural society which evolved to service the developing colonial economy thus consisted of three generalized ethnic divisions: Malay, Chinese and Indian. Though simplistic and ill-defined, these were the categories by which the British administration perceived and governed local society" (Andaya and Andaya, 1982, p. 180).

***

Kuala Lumpur

The junction of the Klang and Gombak rivers grew into Kuala Lumpur from about 1857, although there were earlier Malay villages in nearby locations along the banks of the Klang. It was in 1857 that Raja Abdullah, who then controlled the Klang valley, sent a large party of Chinese miners, assembled with the backing of S.S. merchants, to the river junction. The junction became the base from which miners searched for tin. The substantial investment which prospecting and mining required was funded variously by Malay, Chinese and British interests.

At the rivers' junction incoming labourers and supplies were unloaded and outgoing tin ore loaded. Hakka Chinese traders set up shop on the eastern bank of the Klang river and a primitive village built with local timber and thatch began to grow; although until the late 1870s it was a mere shanty town for trading, three days upstream by boat from Klang. Malays settled to the left and Chinese to the right of an area on the east bank which became a central square, nowadays Leboh Pesar Besar but formerly Market Square. The emerging town suffered a severe setback during the 1867–1873 Selangor "civil war" which, as we have seen, was the proximate cause of British intervention in Selangor immediately after the Pangkor Engagement. However, after 1873, recovery was rapid, in no small way due to the energy of the Capitan China, Yap Ah Loy. Swettenham, as Assistant Resident in 1875, wrote that the emergent Kuala Lumpur was "by far the best mining village I have seen, the streets wide and excellently arranged, the shops most substantial … in front of the Captain's house are the Gambling Booths and the Market … there are about 1,000 Chinese in the town and some 500 to 700 Malays" (Gullick, 1994, p. 7).

A slump in the price of tin between 1875 and 1879 made the survival of Kuala Lumpur precarious. Its main investor, Yap Ah Loy, struggled to service loans at 15% or more for his incoming supplies. He had borrowed in both Singapore and Malacca, not only from Chinese merchants but also from Guthrie & Co. and the Selangor government, paying interest up to 20% on 6–12 month terms (Gullick, 1983, p. 27). It was feared that his merchant creditors would call a halt, bring him to bankruptcy and force closure of the mines. But the tin market turned around dramatically in late 1879, with the world price of tin rising by one-third in a single month. The ensuing boom brought in more labourers and the population of Kuala Lumpur grew by a third in one year. The increasing numbers led to hygiene and health problems and outbreaks of fire, to say nothing of the further threat to the town posed by frequent flooding of the rivers.

In 1880, the S.S. government in Singapore decided that the Resident of Selangor, Bloomfield Douglas, and his officials, should move to Kuala Lumpur as a more fitting seat of authority than Klang. Douglas' tenure there was not happy. He was distrusted by the Singapore officials and lacked the confidence of the Malay chiefs; there was also suspicion that he profited from land speculation. When Governor Weld inspected the town in 1882 he was displeased with both the condition of the town and

Douglas' administration. Douglas resigned in August 1882 and Swettenham succeeded him as resident of Selangor (Barr, 1977, pp. 63–67).

Swettenham set about to shake things up and rebuild the entire town. He quickly spent money on public works and social needs. He gave a high priority to roads and paths and streets were cleared and rebuilt with front-ages moved back so as to make the roads wider: "stretches of the paths were made wide enough for bullock-carts which carried food, timber and charcoal to the camps and tin from the mines to the river outlets" (Barr, 1977, p. 69). The passable thoroughfares also brought from inland small traders who set up stalls selling jungle fruits. The zealous Resident acti-vated the Public Works Department into developing saleable plots of land, improving the water supply, relocating the slaughter houses remotely out of town and cleaning up the filthy brothels. Swettenham did not even neglect the prison — ensuring that prisoners had adequate facilities for baths with soap and water — or the hospital, with the provision of extra bedding, a new pharmacist and private facilities for the surgeon.

After the death of Yap Ah Loy in 1885, the market square was also cleared and a new Central Market built on the open space. On visiting Kuala Lumpur in 1886, Governor Weld reported favourably on the improvements: "picturesque houses and shops brightly painted and often ornamented with carving and gilding." (Gullick, 1983, p. 43; 1994, p. 14.) However, the Europeans settled not among the Chinese and Malays on the east but across the river on its western bank. To link the two halves of the town it was necessary to bridge the river in several places.

The next step was to construct a railway connection between Kuala Lumpur and Klang. The line was opened in 1886, much to the delight of octogenarian Sultan Abdul Samed who became "something of a railway buff" as a result of his first ride to Klang (Gullick, 1994, p. 15). By 1909, a north–south line ran from Penang to Singapore with several western connections. Kuala Lumpur was the centre of the rail network and con-tained the railway workshops and administration.

In the 19th century there was only a handful of British businessmen in Kuala Lumpur, notably Archie C. Harper (formerly inspector of police), who founded the firm which became Harper Gilfillan, and J.A. Russell of the eponymous company. In 1888 the Chartered Bank set up agencies in Kuala Lumpur and Taiping but their business did not go much beyond granting small loans to petty traders and contractors. A proposal in 1891 to establish another agency in the new port of Telok Anson was knocked on the head by London Head Office (Mackenzie, 1954, p. 215). Not until the turn of the century did British merchant firms and banks begin to commit seriously to Kuala Lumpur.

Meanwhile, improvements to Kuala Lumpur continued. By the 1890s its population was some 20,000. In Chinatown, shop-houses replaced single-storey buildings, thus providing for both residence and trade on a narrow plot of land. The well-to-do of all communities built grander residences outside the town, to the west and the north-east along Ampang road. Adjacent to the Padang (nowadays Merdeka Square) the European officials and merchants built the government offices, the Chartered Bank, St Mary's Church and the Selangor Club. The development of the Lake Gardens began in the 1880s on the initiative of Alfred Venning, the State treasurer, with the support of European and Chinese colleagues and notables. The Indian community was also growing in number, wealth and standing. Its leaders were men of commerce and moneylending. They built their houses north of the town.

***

On the retirement in 1889 of Hugh Low as Resident of Perak, that post was given to Frank Swettenham and William Maxwell succeeded him in Selangor. Both states thrived. In his very different style, Maxwell was as zealous for progress as his rival Swettenham. Maxwell spent almost 30 years in Malaya, devoted to his work and to historical and cultural scholarship of the country. He was most able and of complete integrity; but he was imperious, overbearing, feared by his subordinates and "a little rough and hasty" with the Malays. Maxwell was "a disciplinarian who set the highest standards for himself and had a poor view of human frailties in others. [Swettenham] was less of an idealist; more willing to compromise; more tolerant of his fellow men … popular with the Malays as well as with British officials" (Thio, 1969, p. 157; see also Gullick, 1983, pp. 58–59).

Maxwell began in Selangor with a massive reorganisation of land administration, a subject which previously he had studied in South Australia and administered in the S.S. The reform in Selangor was accompanied by a clean-up of dubious land-trafficking by government officials, in which the most luckless victim was Spence Moss, the engineer who had built the railway line between Kuala Lumpur and Klang (Gullick, 1983, pp. 58–59).

British administrators in the protected states offered financial incentives to pioneers who would develop plantation agriculture on the peninsula: 999-year leases at very low prices together with government loans. These favourable terms were drawn up by Maxwell when he was Assistant Resident to Low in Perak. "Among the chief takers were Ambrose Rathborne and his partner Heslop Hill whose names figure prominently in the Agricultural Concessions lists of the 1880s, and who acquired 8,000 acres of land in Selangor almost rent free and 12,000 more in Perak at 50 cents an acre and no rent" (Barr, 1977, p. 92). Guthrie & Co. also assisted Rathborne with finance.

Rathborne was a pioneer coffee planter — having previously abandoned the same occupation in Ceylon when coffee was blighted by fungal disease. When management of coffee estates on the peninsula became beset by labour shortage and difficulties in the 1880s, Rathborne turned to road building under Swettenham in Selangor. The coffee plantations had their ups and downs, including a boom period in the late 1880s and early 1890s consequent on a rise in coffee prices and alleviation of the labour problems by the importation of docile Tamil labourers from South India. "By the end of 1893 there were 19 European-owned estates totalling some 12,300 acres in Selangor, nearly all around Kuala Lumpur and Klang and nearly all concentrating on the cultivation of Liberian coffee" (Barr, 1977, p. 116). However, competition from Brazil eventually made coffee cultivation unviable and the plantations were turned over to rubber trees — of which more in subsequent chapters.

The Federation of Malay States

The idea of a federation of the protected states — with a Resident-General as the administrative superior — had been around since at least the early 1880s. In 1885, C.P. Lucas of the Colonial Office had thought that the invaluable Hugh Low of Perak might also be given oversight of Residents of the other states. Low himself, in a memorandum to the Colonial Office prior to his retirement from Perak in 1889, thought that the four states should be confederated, so as to ensure uniformity of policy and to allow surplus funds to be shifted from the richer states to aid the development of the poorer. In 1891, W.E. Maxwell, then Resident of Selangor, touted those ideas in a speech at the Royal Colonial Institute; and in an official memorandum of 1895 he said that it was absurd that there should be multiple state departments doing work which could be done consistently and more efficiently by a single department for each administrative function.

Success has many fathers and the parentage of the eventual Federation was claimed by many British officials, especially Swettenham. The emergence of the Federation concept and its eventual achievement has been discussed in great detail (Sadka, 1968; Thio, 1969) and succinctly (Andaya and Andaya, 1982; Barr, 1977), so it need only be summarised here.

Matters were brought to a head in the early 1890s by the huge financial difficulties of Pahang and, to a lesser extent, Negri Sembilan. The S.S. had sanctioned loans to those poorer states during the 1880s in the expectation that such assistance would increase trade and investment opportunities (in which prospects various merchants in the S.S. had interests; although up to 1895 there had been no large-scale influx of European capital). However, the S.S. encountered a trade depression in 1890–1892, had to deal with demands from London for an increased contribution towards local defence needs and, at the same time, suffered a fall of 25% in the exchange value of the Straits dollar against the pound sterling. The S.S. could no longer afford to be lenient to Pahang and the Negri Sembilan. It was thought that the wealth of Perak and Selangor could be tapped to assist the weaker states if a federation of the four states could be achieved (see especially Sadka, 1968, pp. 364–386).

Ever the man to seize the hour, Swettenham, then Resident of Perak, set about obtaining approval from the Malay State Rulers for a F.M.S.:

> *Having discussed the matter very thoroughly with the Governor [Sir Charles Mitchell] and with my fellow Residents, I prepared a detailed scheme of reorganization, and drafted a short agreement which, by the Governor's instructions, I took to each of the four Rulers, and to five*

Chiefs of minor states in the Negri Sembilan, and obtained the signa-
tures of all the Malays concerned. (Swettenham, 1942, p. 107; see also
Thio, 1969, pp. 159–162.)

Swettenham was persuasive quickly and the F.M.S. came into being
in July 1896 with Kuala Lumpur as its capital and with its administration
"… headed by a Resident-General with jurisdiction over all the Residents
and authority to represent the Federation's interest to the Singapore
Governor, who was also High Commissioner for the Malay States"
(Andaya and Andaya, 1982, p. 183). No common treasury was established
but, by Article Five of the Treaty of Federation, the Rulers agreed "to give
to those states of the Federation which require it such assistance in men,
money, or other respects as the British Government, through its duly
appointed officers, may advise". Swettenham, who had been far from
disinterested in promoting the Federation, unsurprisingly became its first
Resident-General, which post he held until 1900, before becoming
Governor of the S.S. and High Commissioner for the F.M.S. in 1901.

Under the direction of the Resident-General, F.M.S.-wide departments were created for justice, police, public works, railways, post and
telegraph, surveys and mines, each with a departmental head in Kuala
Lumpur, and all parts of a unified F.M.S. civil service. The consequent
increase in civil service responsibilities and resident personnel gave a
considerable boost to the development and income of Kuala Lumpur; the
centralisation of power was displayed by the grand and handsome
Moorish-style government office buildings completed in 1897 facing the
padang, and intact to the present day. Although something of a stylistic
mixture, described as Neo-Saracenic, the pink brick construction with
three dome towers is very striking and exudes a strong sense of authority
(Gullick, 1994, pp. 27–28 and plates 5, 12, 13; Barr, 1977, p. 125).

Under Swettenham's leadership, the F.M.S. ticked over generally
smoothly and certainly progressively. His credo was, "The country is, to
a great extent, an unpopulated jungle; money must be spent in developing
its resources and men of energy — miners, planters, traders, and
Government servants — must be encouraged to drive the work along"
(Resident-General's report for 1896, quoted by Thio, 1969, p. 179). He
had earlier written that "revenue and prosperity follow the liberal but

prudently-directed expenditure of public funds, especially when they are invested in high-class roads, in railways, telegraphs, waterworks, and everything likely to encourage trade and private enterprise" (in his Perak report 1894, quoted by Sadka, 1968, p. 339). Officials were there "to open up the country by great works: roads, railways, telegraphs, wharves" (reported in the *Straits Budget, 28 April 1896,* quoted by Chai, 1964, p. 66). The Secretary of State for the Colonies, then Joseph Chamberlain, was of a like mind and sanctioned loan-raising by the F.M.S. for ambitious railway construction. Road building was also undertaken and Chinese and European enterprise received great encouragement from the Resident-General. The public works dividend was swift, sure and large: in 1900 the total revenue of the F.M.S. exceeded $15.5 million and the value of their total trade approached $100 million with exports exceeding imports by $10 million (Chai, 1964, p. 65). Nevertheless,

> *Swettenham deplored the lack of British interest in the Malay States and therefore did all he could to attract European investment in mining, planting and building. Large areas of land were granted to prospective planters on favourable terms, loans were advanced to agriculturalists, roads were constructed, banks established, and a more efficient system of justice introduced.* (Thio, 1969, p. 180.)

By the 1903 end of Swettenham's long service in Malaya, the F.M.S. under his leadership had large revenues, money in the bank, no debt, increased population, railways, roads, telegraph lines, hospitals, schools and other public works.

It was, however, a matter of regret that the Malay population had made little material progress, their Rulers had suffered diminished power and authority, and the F.M.S. administrators became much more remote than the state Residents from the Malay population. "In fact, after 1896, more administration was carried out by the Residents in consultation with the Resident-General, without any reference to the ruler of the state or the state council" (Andaya and Andaya, 1982, p. 183). Moreover, as succeeding chapters will show, the Malay population was soon overrun by the immigration of large numbers of Chinese and Indians needed as labour for public works, the growing mining industry and the nascent rubber plantations. Establishment of the Federation virtually coincided with the beginning of the plantation rubber boom and European investment in large-scale tin mining methods:

> *The feature which jumps to the eyes is that federation attracted money to develop agriculture, that the immense foreign capital so introduced brought Indian labour and European planters to control it ... while the old tin industry has undergone great changes, owing to the introduction of modern methods of mining under European direction and paid for by European capital ... [such that the Malay States] ... are no longer the exclusive concern of Malay Rulers and their people, with alien Chinese as the workers and principal taxpayers and a few British officers to direct affairs.* (Swettenham, 1926, p. 8.)

Chapter 5

Currency and Banks

Currency and banking have been described in summary form in the first section of Chapter 2 and touched on variously elsewhere. As there is a very large and rich literature on these subjects, there is no need for any detailed account here. Interested readers may refer to the literature, especially to King (1957), Chiang (1966), Mackenzie (1954) and Drake (1969, 1981, 2004). This chapter therefore deals mainly with matters internal to the two leading banks of the period under review, the Chartered Bank and the Hong Kong and Shanghai Bank (HKSBC).

***

Of major concern to the banks and the merchants was the wide fluctuation in the value of the Straits dollar during the 1890s, between a high of 3s.6d in 1891 and a low of 2s.¼d in 1889. As the dollar fell, exporters benefited but import prices rose in dollar terms, to the disadvantage of Straits residents:

> *The entrepot trade slowed down because of traders' uncertainty about future price movements; but most importantly, the position of persons with debts or commitments in sterling deteriorated noticeably. This affected not only the government, which was committed to a sterling loan, the regular import of supplies, and salaries and pensions payable in sterling, but also private business. Capital inflow was discouraged, because of fears about the rate at which it could be repatriated, and*

most expatriate enterprises had regular sterling obligations for supplies, salaries, etc. In consequence of these effects of silver depreciation, exchange speculation set in against the dollar, thus precipitating a further fall in the exchange rate. (Drake, 1969, pp. 20–21.)

The overriding importance of safeguarding international trade and investment motivated the currency reform of 1903–1906. A Straits Settlements Currency Committee was appointed in 1902 and reported in 1903. It suggested a number of reforms designed to protect the international trade of the Straits from the vagaries of silver price fluctuations. Essentially the aims of the reform measures were to switch the dollar from a silver standard to the gold standard and fix a firm rate of exchange between the dollar and sterling. On 29 January 1906, the government decreed "as from and after the date of this order the Currency Commissioners may issue notes in exchange for gold received by them at Singapore at the rate of sixty dollars for seven pounds sterling", i.e., $1 = 2s.4d. At this date the silver based content of the dollar was valued at 2s.1⅛d, giving a cushion against the melting of silver coinage. The Straits dollar was then notionally on a gold standard. The currency and banking operations thereafter, which the British banks dominated, provided currency for local circulation and full convertibility of Malayan dollar into pounds sterling at all times.

The reformed Malayan monetary system was simple, inexpensive and perfectly suited to a period of development, investment and capital migration.

World War I, which made the shipment of gold dangerous and expensive, caused the Commissioners to throw over completely the form of the gold standard and from then they undertook merely to provide sterling against dollars at the 2s.4d rate. From this point, Malaya was formally on a gold exchange standard (sterling being convertible to gold) until Britain went off the gold standard in 1931, at which point the dollar was on a sterling exchange standard, still at the 2s.4d rate.

The Chartered Bank of India, Australia and China

The Chartered Bank is the subject of a monumental history, *Realms of Silver: One Hundred Years of Banking in the East* (Mackenzie, 1954). The present chapter mainly draws on the Bank's Court Minutes, Internal Letter Books (ILB) and Reports to relate selected details of its activities in the period under review.

In 1858, Mr David Duff of Singapore was appointed to open the Bank's agency there. A credit of £50,000 was arranged through City Bank in favour of the Chartered in Singapore and 50,000 Mexican silver dollars were purchased and shipped there (Court Minutes, 8-9-1858). However, Duff was soon in trouble with the London directors because of exceeding his lending limits, notably advancing $100,000 on the Promissory Note of Syed Abdoullah Ben Omar Al Juneid, whereas his instructions were a limit of £5,000 to any one party (Court Minutes, 2-11-1859). The Bank's Inspector was sent out to examine unauthorised transactions and Duff was dismissed. However, Duff had influence in Singapore and he so persuaded the merchants that he had been unfairly treated that there was a mild run on the Bank, which was thwarted by generous assistance from the Oriental Bank (Mackenzie, 1954, p. 105). C.S. Sherwood was then appointed Singapore agent of the Bank. With approval, he made a large loan of $100,000 to Joshua Brothers, the main importers of opium, under guarantee from Syed Abdoullah (Court Minutes, 1-5-1861).

In 1865, Penang merchants were dissatisfied that there was only one bank on the island, the agency of the Mercantile, and wanted another. Sherwood, now Inspector, was doubtful as he thought that Penang was rather small for two banks. Nevertheless he suggested that capital from the Karachi branch might be invested better in Penang (ILB, 19-6 and 9-10-1865). Sherwood was also concerned about excessive competition in Singapore, where there were four rival bank agencies. There was not enough business in discounts and loans and even exchange operations were not very profitable (ILB, 15-3-1866). In the same long letter, Sherwood noted that the importing of opium was almost entirely in the hands of Joshua Bros. A few months later he reported that Singapore had more money in hand than it could employ; opium was the only good opportunity but it was not favoured by Head Office (ILB, 22-8-1866).

The Bank's standing in Singapore declined, European accounts were reduced to low figures and the Chinese were the only customers who stuck. The Bank's standing was so low that merchant firms were reluctant to deal with it. Head Office wrote to Sherwood that the Court had resolved to reduce the capital of the Singapore branch from £100,000 to £50,000. However, the branch remained well off for local deposits (ILB, 26-12-1866).

Improvement came in 1868 when Bousteads and Guthries renewed the buying of Chartered Bank bills, especially those drawn on Chitties (Indian chettiars). "Although these people were not in every respect those in whom the bank might have complete confidence ... they were none the less shrewd, cunning men of business, and there was no doubt that the Chinamen to whom they sold their opium were very good men generally" (ILB, 11-10-1867). A healthy profit was anticipated for the first half of 1868, helped by the good business of Joshuas who were importing opium daily, and with more on the seas Sherwood thought they should make a profit of $80 a chest. Sherwood also noted a fear that government would tax bank notes issued to the extent of ½% p.a., which was indeed imposed from 1 January 1868. Sherwood reluctantly concluded that the banks would have to make the best of the situation and pay the tax. They would "get no sympathy from the merchants, who were only too glad that revenue could be derived from any source that did not affect themselves" (ILB, 18-1-1868).

By 1872, the opium trade had become risky and the Bank was holding bills of Chinamen and chettiars given against opium purchases totalling $438,851. The price of the drug fluctuated frequently and widely "as had been recently forcibly illustrated in the case of Whampoa, who had been looked upon almost up to the date of his failure as undoubted" (ILB, 4-8-1872). Moreover the Bazaar was not healthy. Chitties were buying piece goods on three months credit and selling them for cash at a loss. By November, Joshua Bros. had failed, owing the Mercantile Bank £125,000 and the Oriental Bank £40,000. Velge Bros. had also failed, owing the Chartered $10,000, the Mercantile $43,000 and the Oriental $15,000 (ILB, 22-11-1872).

The Bank finally decided to open a branch in Penang in 1875 (Court Minutes, 7-10-1874). Inspector Simpson made an extensive report on the Singapore branch in 1878, indicating that it undoubtedly did the largest banking business in Singapore with good results. Local business was the chief source of profit. Simpson observed that manager Neave's long residence in Singapore and his intimate acquaintance with native firms made him especially suitable for handling local business. However, the Bank's premises were much too small and although the lease was not due to expire until 1882, Simpson thought it possible that a suitable house might become available for purchase (ILB, 30-9-1878). By this time a full branch under Budd was in business at Penang and noted favourably by Simpson (ILB, 7-12-1878).

In 1880, Inspector T.J. Mullins came from Hong Kong to report on the Singapore branch. He noted that the bulk of promissory notes were signed by Chinese and endorsed over to Chitties, who discounted them at the Bank. This represented money borrowed by the Chinese from the Chitties for trade purposes. Neave's long experience in Singapore stood the Bank in good stead. Overdrafts totalled $517,799 of which about half were for shipments of produce by Gilfillan Wood & Co., Maclaine Fraser & Co., Martin Dyce & Co., Paterson Simons & Co., Puttfarcken Rheiner & Co., and Reine Bros. The biggest of these accounts was G.W. & Co. which, however, gave exchange business to the Chartered only when its rates compared favourably with other banks. Mullins thought that G.W. & Co. should give the Chartered all their exchange business when the rate difference against the other banks was only $\frac{1}{8}\%$. Mullins declared that "the Branch was the most popular institution of its kind in Singapore and its senior officers were looked up to and respected by the whole community" (ILB, 23-4-1880).

In Penang, the Bank's business with the Chitties was different from that in Singapore. The Penang Chitties dealt with the Chinese in promissory notes and they also gave advances on the security of title deeds. The Bank gave advances to the Penang Chitties at interest rates from $9\frac{1}{2}\%$ to 11% p.a., always on the basis of two borrower signatures:

> *Penang was increasingly prosperous. It was the centre of the tin mining and tobacco areas. Perak and Selangor all sent their tin to Penang and were supplied in return with Coolies, Stores, Piece Goods, etc. ... Many of the Chinese had become extremely wealthy and had invested in land and house property with the result that values of property in the settlement had risen considerably over the years. (ILB, 22-5-1883.)*

Mullins had a high opinion of the Chitties and in 1885 wrote:

> *There was no question of them subsequently remitting cover and they should not be classed as mere speculators in exchange. The Chitties have money laid down in India as well as in the Straits and would have little difficulty in realizing it if necessary. When from their point of view the price of Rupees was low in the Straits they considered it suited them to draw on India and invest the proceeds in the Straits and when high they would await the opportunity to remit.*

Chitties, Chettys and Chettiars are a caste of financiers from South India and are ubiquitous in Southeast Asia (Cunyngham-Brown, 1971, p. 156 note).

Penang branch was always short of money, and that enabled the HKSBC, which opened in the Straits in 1877, to secure a large share of business. Mullins thought that Head Office should enlarge the Bank's reserves in both Penang and Singapore so that it could buy more sterling to compete with the HKSBC. Although Penang had large fixed deposits, principally from the governments of Perak and Penang, these deposits represented security given by the opium farmers for performance of their contracts and the deposits were committed to that purpose; so these funds did not enlarge the branch's loanable funds for other uses (ILB, Penang, 15-5-1886).

Singapore branch was also under heavy competition from the HKSBC for sterling exchange business. Head Office believed that the weakening of the Chartered's previous grip on the exchange business was to an extent due to the inadequacies of Mr Dougal, then manager in Singapore. Dougal admitted that the HKSBC had cut into his business. However, Mullins wrote that the rival bank had become a great power in Singapore. It had enormous and overwhelming strength in China; it allowed almost unlimited freedom to its Singapore manager; it ran great risks to secure constituents from other banks, preferably the Chartered; its manager's hospitality was lavish; and there was an entire absence of those restrictions which other banks imposed on their Singapore managers (ILB, 24-4-1885). He also thought that the Chartered had lost popularity in the time of Dougal's predecessor, Wallace, but Dougal had restored it so far as the British firms were concerned.

The Sultan of Johore was a large borrower from the Bank, owing some $491,000 of the Bank's total fixed loans of $577,000. The loan to the Sultan was to be repaid by monthly instalments and it was secured by property valued at $500,000, part of which the bank occupied. The HKSBC continued to put great competitive pressure on other banks by offering money to the Singapore Municipality at 5% p.a. and to private borrowers at 7%. The Chartered reduced its overdraft rate to 8% in both Singapore and Penang but had to give the New Harbour Dock Co. 7% on its overdraft, while Paterson Simons & Co. were seeking 6% (ILB, 16-4-1886). The Hong Kong bank drew great strength from its China connections and the fact that that many Chinese in Singapore were attached to it. The Hong Kong branch of the HKSBC repeatedly shipped silver dollar coin to Singapore so that its branch there was flush with loanable funds, whereas the Chartered in Singapore received only one shipment of Mexican silver dollars in half the year; therefore it was impossible to compete with the HKSBC in the purchase of sterling bills (ILB, 8-5-1886).

In 1891, Head Office thought that in Penang there was too much money in local advances and not enough for exchange business. Local advances were to be curtailed within limits of $1,000,000 for the Chinese and $200,000 for the Chitties (Inspectors Book II, 5-6-1891).

The Bank opened a sub-agency in Kuala Lumpur in 1888, which was the first bank representation there. In November of the same year, another sub-agency was opened in Taiping. W.A. Main, the acting manager in Singapore, was to see that advances on town leases and other immobile security were discontinued at Kuala Lumpur but otherwise the sub-agency was not troubled (ILB, 19-6-1891). Taiping, however, was troublesome for some years. Its early results were disappointing but Head Office decided to persevere rather than open at Telok Anson. Taiping made loans to government officials, one of whom was borrowing from the Bank at 9% p.a. and relending to Chinese at 18% p.a. (ILB, 22-5-1891). This was frowned upon and eventually attracted attention at the Colonial Office in 1895. After correspondence with the Colonial Office the Court decided that Taiping, which was making losses, should be closed; but that decision was reversed within three months (ILB, 27-3-1895, 13-11-1895 and 5-2-1896).

The Sultan of Johore's good standing with the Bank was demonstrated by an additional $40,000 loan in 1893, reductions of his interest rate to 7% p.a. in 1894 and to 6% p.a. in 1895 and a further loan of $250,000 guaranteed by Paterson Simons & Co. (Court Minutes, 23-8-1893, 27-12-1894, 2-10-1895 and 23-4-1902). The Court also reviewed the loan limits of many merchant firms (Court Minutes, various, 1894).

The Bank habitually charged the Straits Trading Co. a small commission on silver shipped on their account to Perak. This apparently was a continual irritation to the company and Main thought that the commission should be waived and the Bank be content with the interest charged on the Straits Trading Co. overdrafts at Penang and Singapore. It was also proposed to reduce the interest rate paid on current account balances in Singapore but it was feared that the HKSBC would not do the same (ILB, Malaya General, 13-3-1895 and 23-3-1895). The Penang limit for advances to Chitties was increased to $300,000 and subsequently to $500,000 (Court Minutes, 29-1-1896 and 14-9-1898).

By 1899, the Bank was finding it difficult to employ funds in Singapore, Penang, Kuala Lumpur and Taiping. Government Fixed Deposits were piling up while at the same time there was a large falling off in sales of Rupees and Sterling, so the branches had more local money than could be utilized (Half-Yearly Reports, 1899). Singapore's large cash balances and the interest payable locally on fixed deposits and current accounts told heavily against profits; the year had been extremely favourable to importers and produce prices were high, so the merchants were flush with deposit funds.

The Bank opened an agency in Ipoh in 1902, which displeased the Straits Trading Co. which hitherto had been the only means of making remittances from Ipoh. Fixed Deposits at Penang fell considerably due to withdrawals by the Federated Malay States (F.M.S.) government, but at Kuala Lumpur the government opened a fresh current account on which 1% p.a. interest was allowed (Half Yearly Report, Singapore, July 1903). The F.M.S. government by then was opening up vast tracts of waste land for rice cultivation, with irrigation works being prepared at Krian, and rubber planting continued on a large scale. However, "the only drawback was that Chinese would not take up land cultivation so long as mining remained profitable" (Half Yearly Report, Singapore, January 1903). Ipoh was the centre of the tin mining district where 70,000 coolies were employed; the Bank was trying to work its way with the Chinese, hoping to command the bulk of their business in the Kinta district (Half Yearly Report, Penang, July 1903).

Agreement was reached with the Straits Trading Co. whereby the Bank undertook to provide their requirements at ¹⁄₁₆% p.a. commission and the company would cease all lending and exchange operations (Half Yearly Report, Penang, July 1903). The Penang limit for Chitties was raised to $750,000 and the Singapore limit for Chinese to $250,000 (Court Minutes, 14-9-1904 and 17-2-1904).

Singapore had surplus funds early in 1905 but it was not thought wise to discourage deposits as it was anticipated that the surplus would be very useful once the currency question was fixed (Half Yearly Report, Singapore, January 1905). Six months later there were numerous failures in the Bazaar and the Bank was forced to curtail much hitherto lucrative business. Failures were estimated at $5 million of which Chitties lost $3 million. Business was confused and cautious at this time because of uncertainty about exchange fluctuations and currency reform. Moreover, there was keen competition among now eight exchange banks quoting unprofitable rates. On the other hand, rubber production was booming and it was estimated that 30,000 acres on the Malay peninsula had been planted with rubber (Half Yearly Report, Singapore, July 1905). In January 1906, the clouds of uncertainty cleared when the exchange rate was fixed at 2s.4d per dollar on the gold exchange standard.

***

From 1906 a sound currency and stable exchange rate generated great confidence for investment in the Straits Settlements (S.S.) and the F.M.S. The first decade of the 20th century also saw a booming rubber industry. Earlier plantings of rubber trees were now yielding latex, the price of rubber was high and plenty of land was available for plantation development. All that the nascent rubber industry needed was capital and labour. Both were forthcoming. The large merchant firms, now becoming agency houses, promoted the raising of capital by floating new rubber companies on the London stock exchange and British investors took up the shares. Immigration reforms in the F.M.S. allowed for a massive influx of labourers, mostly from southern India. More or less simultaneously, the tin mining industry underwent fundamental technical change as deeper working required very expensive dredges, which were financed by joint stock companies in London.

Ipoh reported that tin mining was flourishing with many new companies and modern machinery. Applications were opened for mining land in Kinta at $25 per acre. The Lands Office at Batu Gajah was inundated with applications (Half Yearly Report, Penang, January 1907). Ipoh town was much improved on the advice of the new Resident, Ernest Woodford Birch.

The tide went out by 1908, after a slump in the price of tin which caused many small mines to shut down. The low price of tin drove the miners to strict economy: coolie wages were reduced by 15–20% and it was hoped that government duty would be lowered from 13% to 10%. Although there was also a fall in the price of rubber, planters reckoned that they could still make profits and indeed much money was still spent on capital works on rubber estates (Half Yearly Report, Penang, January 1908). Three prominent firms — Adamson Gilfillan, Bousteads and Paterson Simons — refused to give Chinese dealers more than two months credit. Some 40 leading Chinese met and informed the merchant firms that two months credit was inadequate and that Dutch firms in Sumatra allowed four months. The Bank in Penang thought that other merchants would not follow the three leaders, who would then be disadvantaged (Half Yearly Report, Penang, January 1909).

The recent depression was illustrated by a dramatic fall in overdrafts to the Chitties from a total (for Penang, Medan, Ipoh and Taiping) of $1,347,000 at 31 December 1907 to $323,000 at 31 December 1909. The Chitties also claimed that they could get plenty of money from India, on cheaper terms and with easier security conditions, than in Penang (Half Yearly Report, Penang, January 1910). Six months later, the tide came in again. Consumer expenditure was increasing rapidly, as a consequence of increased immigrant labour on the rubber estates. Prosperity returned and in the end 1910 was a good year for exporters and importers. Bousteads was said to have record profits on each side of trade. The price of tin was soaring,

> *and there is no other branch of our export business which has such an improving effect on local trade and the prosperity of people in this part of the World. The whole money proceeds of the exports of tin is said to*

go into the pockets of the local populace, whereas in the case of say rub-
ber the money goes into the pockets of the company shareholders in
Europe and elsewhere. (Half Yearly Report, Penang, July 1911.)

The large increases in deposits led to large amounts paid out in deposit interest. Penang recorded poor results for this reason and also from losses in exchange. Inspector Thomas Henderson Whitehead commented that this was a "deplorable example of bad finance and bad judgment in Exchange" (Half Yearly Report, Penang, January 1912).

Although World War I caused little damage to Straits trade, as tin and rubber were essential commodities for military materials, the Penang branch found fewer Bills offering because the Straits Trading Co. was selling tin in Singapore, where the smelting facilities at Pulo Brani had been improved. The Eastern Smelting Co. was also selling tin in Singapore as well as large amounts in London. However, it was hoped that tin exports from Penang would revive after the completion of Eastern Smelting's new works at Butterworth. A further blow to Penang was the fact that rubber was also going to Singapore for auction (Half Yearly Report, Penang, July 1915). The development of rubber plantations continued apace during the war, especially in Kedah where transport improvements facilitated increased production. There was therefore a need for bank services in both Sungei Patani and Alor Star. The Land Office of Kedah asked the three British banks if they would open in Sungei Patani where, if so, the Kedah government would alienate a suitable office site on reasonable terms. However, the Chartered's manager at Penang declined the offer because the Bank would be too short of staff until after the war (Half Yearly Report, Penang, January 1918).

The Hong Kong and Shanghai Banking Corporation

There is a substantial four-volume history of the Bank by Frank King in which Volume II (1988) contains only limited reference to the S.S. and Malay States in our period of interest. The present section mainly draws on Internal Letter Books for the year 1908, the only year for which correspondence concerning the Bank's branches in the S.S. was available to me. Thus the HKSBC sources do not deal with Singapore and Malaya as fully as do those of the Chartered Bank.

The HKSBC opened an agency in Singapore in 1877, which developed into a branch with an "outport" agency in Penang. By 1908, the Singapore manager was the "energetic and ambitious" T.S. Baker who was keen for expansion. In 1910 the Bank moved into Ipoh and Kuala Lumpur to secure the business its Penang agency had developed on the peninsula, and to Malacca to serve planter interests. The Malacca venture, "encouraged by the Straits Settlements Governor, Sir John Anderson, was facilitated by the offer of temporary accommodation and the deposit of government funds". The Government of the F.M.S. in Kuala Lumpur also promised a share of its business. In the same year the Bank opened a sub-agency in Johore Bahru to cement a long association with the Sultan and his government (King, 1988, p. 35).

Baker was concerned about the governance consequences of unemployed coolies in the Malay States:

> *This is becoming a serious problem. The F.M.S. Govt have asked the Treasurer to send them $500,000 immediately and are making enquiries about borrowing $1,000,000 further, to set to work at once on Roads, Railways and Public Works to keep the Coolies employed until the position of Tin improves. The Coolies are too necessary for the Native States to be repatriated. A few, I am told, are going on to rubber plantations. It is expected that there will be at least 50,000 out of employment by the end of this month.* (T.S. Baker, Singapore, to J.R.M. Smith, Hong Kong, 9 January 1908.)

Another major concern was about the stability of the 2s.4d exchange rate, as the S.S. was in danger of being flooded with silver Straits dollars ousted from Sumatra by the Dutch authorities there. The Straits Treasurer contemplated importing 500,000 gold sovereigns from England to cope with redemptions of the silver dollar, as the Currency Commissioners were then holding only 180,000. The Commissioners had also bought 90,000 sovereigns from Hong Kong. Baker thought that the Commissioners would realise sterling securities held by the Crown Agents in London before selling dollars under 2s.4d. (Baker, Singapore to Kilpatrick, Batavia, 13 January 1908; and to Smith, Hong Kong, 8 February 1908).

However, the Straits Government weakened to the extent of selling sterling T.T. at 2s.⅞d pence. Baker rightly believed that the transaction was in breach of the Currency Ordinance and established a precedent which would be prejudicial to the 2s.4d exchange rate. "If Govt work in this erratic manner and give Banks outside the Colony preferential rates for sovereigns we shall never know where we are with our exchange or what they won't do next!" (Baker, Singapore, to Smith, Hong Kong, 8 February 1908.)

A month later, Baker wrote:

As regards maintaining the Straits Exchange I still adhere to the opinion that Govt will not sell the surplus Straits dollars at a sacrifice as long as they have securities at home to sell T.T. against, or any gold here to give in exchange for notes. The position at present is that they have some £600,000 in securities and £125,000 in the Treasury here; and the Note Circulation of the Colony and the F.M.S. is down to $21,319,970 — the lowest it has been since April two years ago just after the 2/4d standard was fixed. (Baker, Singapore to H.E.R. Hunter, Hong Kong, 19 March 1908.)

At this time the Bazaar was tight for money; failures were feared and did occur. Sin Ghee Choon & Co. had an overdraft of almost $30,000 from the Bank but their rich guarantor, Foo Choo Choon was rumoured to be in difficulties. Cecil Guinness, the Relieving Manager in Singapore, reported that the International Bank was closing its offices in Singapore and Penang "owing to the slackness of trade and the number of Banks in the Straits" (Guinness, Singapore to Smith, Hong Kong, 3 May 1908). Worse was to come. Pertile & Co. in Singapore, identical with Schiffmann Heer & Co. of Penang, failed, losing $238,304. The bank was owed $92,042 on overdraft against which it held as security 714 shares in Straits Trading Co. valued at $35,900. Guinness feared that stocks in Singapore and Penang would not be realisable at book values and that Bazaar debts would only be collected slowly and with great difficulty.

Baker was back on duty in June and repeated that business in both Singapore and Penang was in a very bad state. He was curtailing the Bank's advances to Guthrie & Co. He noted that the Chartered Bank was calling up advances, perhaps injudiciously (Baker, Singapore to Smith,

Hong Kong, 12 June 1908). He wrote also to Guinness in Penang warning him to keep down advances to Guthries and informing him that Behn Meyer & Co. and Behr & Co. had agreed to mortgage properties to the Bank as security (Baker, Singapore to Guinness, Penang, 13 June 1908).

The Selangor Spirit and Gambling Farm, which had been let out by Government was not paying its way and so the Government reduced the terms payment. Baker thought that the position of the farmers was unlikely to improve and advised Guinness to have accounts of the farmers paid off or be well secured. He reported that Greig of Bousteads believed it would be disastrous for Penang if Government enforced full payment in terms of the original agreement (Baker, Singapore to Guinness, Penang, 16 June 1908).

In his Half Yearly Report, Baker noted net profits in both Singapore and Penang despite large allocations to the Contingent account to cover probable losses on China exchange contracts. He asserted that any such losses would not be due to rash speculations but simply to the extremely bad times prevailing in the Straits in the past six months and the difficulty Chinese have experienced in collecting accounts. For instance, Liang Moh, the principal delinquent whose total liabilities in Singapore were about $120,000, was $17,000 short on a contract on Shanghai (Baker, Singapore to Smith, Hong Kong, 8 July 1908). Goh Seng suspended payment; he had over $1 million in China contracts outstanding, divided among the German bank, the Mercantile and the Trader, and the loss was some $120,000. Several other Chinese firms which speculated in exchange were troubled but the HKSBC had no interest in any of them. The F.M.S. Government bought the Sungei Ujong Railway for $9 lacs (1 lac = $100,000) and paid for it by withdrawing $4 lacs from Fixed Deposits at Penang branch and $5 lacs from the Chartered Bank. Adamson Gilfillan & Co., as agents of the Railway Co., remitted the money to London with four banks taking shares of it. "We took £35,000 thus replacing the bulk of what had been withdrawn from us from F/Deposit" (Baker, Singapore to Smith, Hong Kong, 30 July 1908).

The trade statistics for the first half year showed a heavy fall in value compared to 1907; this was entirely a matter of price as the quantities of staple exports considerably exceeded the quantities shipped in the same period of 1907. The Chitties' business was very poor in the Straits, due to the general depression and the doubtful financial condition of the Chinese.

A large trader, Fook Yuen, was boycotted by other Chinese in the Straits and Hong Kong for secretly trading in Japanese goods (Baker, Singapore to Smith, Hong Kong, 11 September 1908).

Lo Kee Seng, merchants of Singapore and Canton, asked the Bank for an overdraft of up to $150,000, promising to give the Bank preference in their exchange business with China, as well as property mortgages for security (Baker, Singapore to J.C. Peter, Hong Kong, 24 December 1908). Sarkies Brothers, the noted hoteliers, sought an advance from Penang of up to $120,000 in order to buy the Eastern and Oriental Hotel which they were operating on lease. But the lessor, Lim Soo Chee, already had an advance of $80,000 against the hotel from the Penang office. Nevertheless, Baker wished to give Sarkies the requested advance. He pointed out to Head Office that the Sarkies Bros already ran four large hotels: Raffles in Singapore and the Eastern and Oriental in Penang on lease; and The Crag Hotel on Penang Hill and The Strand Hotel in Rangoon which they owned. As well as giving good security, the Sarkies would transfer the Raffles Hotel current account to the Bank if the advance was given. Baker recommended the advance "in view of the present plethora of money everywhere and there appearing to be no risk in making the advance" (Baker, Singapore to Peter, Hong Kong, 23 October 1908). However, Head Office did not agree, as they were not interested in large advances against hotels and did not want to lock up a large sum for an indefinite period (Baker, Singapore to Guinness, Penang, 11 November 1908).

The Straits Government courted unpopularity with the banks with a plan to lower the rate at which the Currency Commissioners would buy sterling by $5/16$d:

The ostensible object is to establish a Gold Reserve in London instead of Singapore against Notes issued here, but the real object is to enable the Colonial Treasurer in his dual capacity of Currency Commissioner and Colonial Treasurer to dovetail the requirements of the F.M. States and the S.S. Govt with the operations of the Currency Department in issuing notes here against gold in London, thus depriving the Banks of all the exchange business of the F.M. States Govt and the S.S. Govt and rendering the import and export of gold to and from the Straits practically impossible. (Baker, Singapore to Smith, Hong Kong, 5 November 1908.)

In other words, the Banks would never be able to attract business outside the rate at which anyone could deal directly with the Commissioners (Drake, 1969, p. 25 explains how the limits of the exchange spread allowed to the Commissioners were set by the gold import and export points).

The Bank analysed the financial reports of several leading merchant firms. Paterson Simons & Co. was regarded as sound but their limit was to be set at £50,000. McAlister & Co. was thought to have a weak balance sheet, with large Goodwill and small Capital; but the Bank thought their trading business was good enough to retain their custom. Boustead & Co. suffered a large loss in Penang but they held enough realisable security (Baker, Singapore to J.C. Nicholson, London, 16 December 1908).

Baker's instinct was always to be oversold in silver because of the insatiable appetite for it in China (Baker, Singapore to Smith, Hong Kong, 18 December 1908). However, in a fortnight he reversed that strategy and became overbought in silver because of a 4% rise in the price of silver in the interim (Baker, Singapore to Smith, Hong Kong, 1 January 1909).

Business in the Straits was slack in the second half of 1907 and throughout 1908, causing the Bank to tighten its willingness to accept personal guarantees as security for loans, even if the guarantors were men of means. Money was tight in the native Bazaar and merchants were having difficulty in collecting their debts. No failures were reported though there was anxiety about Heng Moh & Co., "one of the oldest established Piece Goods dealers in the Bazaar and always done a large and remunerative business, working principally with Boustead & Co.". The Bank's compradore feared that if Heng Mo & Co. failed they would not pay more than 30% (Guinness, Penang to Baker, Singapore, 18 February 1908). And fail they did, owing the HKSBC $10,905 in exchange contracts. The largest creditor was Boustead & Co. for $60,000. The total liabilities of Heng Moh & Co. were $339,500 and visible assets only about $68,000. The firm's bad and doubtful debts were $250,000 of which only $20,000 was thought recoverable. "The Bazaar here is in a very bad state and it is feared that should many of the dealers be pressed for a settlement there would be a general collapse" (Guinness, Penang to G.C. Murray, Singapore, 5 June 1908).

The next Half Yearly Report from Penang indicated that the branch had done well by increasing advances against produce, and so both Interest Received and Remittances to London increased accordingly. However, it was noted that very severe losses were made by the Chinese through speculation in tin. Stringency in the money market made it very difficult to collect money; consequently those merchants who had exchange contracts outstanding were in many cases unable to take them up:

> *One beneficial result will be that with the late experience none of the Banks will be anxious to make contracts for such long options for delivery but will content themselves with supplying the ready demand as it arises, in this case we can depend on getting the greater portion of the business without running the risk of fluctuations in the silver market.*

The tin market improved but prices of other exports fell so low that the planters were losing money on all products. The Bazaar was in a bad state with many piece goods dealers suspending payment:

> *It is found that when a firm suspends payment the only people acknowledged as such are weak men and the men of means who have formerly been looked upon as partners repudiate all responsibility. The consequence of all this trouble is that merchants have their godowns filled with stocks which they can only get rid of if they are prepared to sell on credit, but they prefer to do no business rather than run the risk of losses until confidence is again restored.* (Guinness, Penang to Chief Manager, Hong Kong, 20 July 1908.)

Guinness wrote very favourably of Tsiang Lee & Co. which enjoyed an advance of $46,000 guaranteed by Khoo Thean Po, backed up by a second mortgage on a 525-acre estate in Province Wellesley. The firm was very well-managed and did a large import business with the Bank's assistance. They acted very prudently in cancelling import orders during the trade depression. From the Bank's viewpoint the firm was quite sound; they met all their bills when due and were not listed as creditors of the many firms that failed (Guinness, Penang to Baker, Singapore, 7 September 1908).

The Bank was well-established in Malaya by 1914, maintaining 25 European staff in the S.S. and the F.M.S.

Other British Banks

Actually, the first British bank in the S.S. was the Oriental Bank Corporation. It had been established at Bombay in 1842 and received its Royal Charter in 1851. The granting of the Charter was most beneficial and led to a 50% increase in the Bank's share price on the London Stock Exchange (Mackenzie, 1954, pp. 9–10). The Bank opened in Singapore in 1846 and became known among the Malays and Chinese as "Bank Besar". It was for a time very successful. At the end of 1862 a dividend of 5% with a bonus of 3% was declared, which with a previous interim dividend made a total payment to shareholders of 15% for the year. The Chairman stated that in 12 years the shareholders had been paid back the whole of the Capital and a further 60%. "It is a pity that it did not go on in this way, and there was a very considerable stir in Singapore in 1884, when it stopped payment" (Buckley, 1965, p. 702). The bank was reincarnated as the New Oriental Banking Corporation but closed finally in 1892 because of losses incurred through the depreciation of silver (Allen and Donnithorne, 1954, p. 203).

The Chartered Mercantile Bank of India, London and China (as it was originally known) opened in Singapore in 1855, at Penang in 1860 and Malacca in 1882. It sought successfully to build business with Guthries, Bousteads and Paterson Simons as well as with local Chinese and Chettiars. It also got a share of government banking business by paying 3% interest on 1882 on government deposits. The Chinese, however, were reluctant to open current accounts despite the offer of 2% interest on deposits (Muirhead, 1996, pp. 224–225). Business was good in Penang but it was watched very carefully by the compradore, and the branch kept in mind that "the head office view generally on business with the Cantonese firms in Penang was that 'it should be carried on with great caution and to moderate or small amounts'" (*ibid.*, p. 226).

The Bank, in common with British banks everywhere at that time, avoided long-term loans. Its policy was trade finance and not capital loans. However, between it did make an advance for the construction of the Sungei Ujong Railway (*ibid.*, p. 231).

One other British bank emerged in the early 20th century, the Eastern Bank which was founded by E.D. Sassoon & Co. and others to work in China (Mackenzie, 1954, p. 207). Not until 1928 did it open in Singapore and so falls outside our period. Nevertheless, it may be worth noting that the Eastern was later absorbed by the Chartered, as was the Mercantile by the HKSBC (Drake, 1969, p. 108).

***

During our period of interest, the Chartered was the premier bank in Malaya, although pressed hard by the competitive HKSBC from the late 19th century. The Chartered was the greater in exchange business, while the HKSBC was able to draw on its huge deposits base in China to pursue broader business in loans and advances (Nishimura *et al.*, 2012, p. 60). The two institutions dominated banking in the S.S. and the Malay States, notwithstanding the substantial business of the lesser Mercantile Bank and the early 20th century emergence of Chinese and other banks.

To conclude, the Chartered Bank was not only predominant in our period, it was also the only British bank firmly anchored in the S.S. As such, it was the first port of call for merchant firms and for the S.S. and F.M.S. governments and their respective staff members. Both the HKSBC and the Mercantile were China institutions which expanded into the S.S. and then into the Malay States. It is no adverse reflection on the abilities and success of these banks to affirm that they were less important than the Chartered in Malayan development during our period.

Chapter 6

Rapid Economic Growth and Change, 1896–1914

By the early 20th century, the underpinnings of a prosperous Malayan export economy were largely in place. The British had "sought and achieved the 'congenial political and administrative framework' in which private enterprise could flourish" (Andaya and Andaya, 1982, p. 207). The administrative and commercial hub was in Singapore but the production of exports was done mostly on the peninsula. Trade was greatly facilitated by substantial infrastructure development and improvement. Singapore's port, which by 1903 was the world's seventh largest in shipping tonnage, was greatly inadequate and desperately in need of modernisation. In 1905, the government expropriated the Tanjong Pagar Dock Co. and created the publicly-owned Tanjong Pagar Dock Board which in 1913 was converted into the Singapore Harbour Board. In the few intervening years, old wharves were replaced, new roads and godowns built, modern equipment installed, a wet dock constructed and electric power introduced. The Harbour Board became the most important public utility in Singapore (Turnbull, 1977, p. 95).

On the peninsula, between 1885 and 1895, four short east–west railway lines had been built on the west coast in order to link tin-fields to ports; in 1901 these lines were amalgamated to form the Federated Malay States Railways; in 1903 a north–south trunk line, paid for entirely out of the revenue of the Federated Malay States (F.M.S.), was constructed to join the inland mining towns and by 1910 it ran from Prai in the north to Johore Bahru in the south. The railway construction further encouraged mining by lowering its costs. The railways returned multiplied talents to the Government in the form of more tin duty as well as their own revenues.

The early British administrators of the Malay States were very anxious for agricultural development and did their best to promote it. They aimed for a prosperous *resident* community of planters and farmers — European and Asian, settlers and indigenes. For example, Frank Swettenham suggested the introduction of Chinese rice growers *with their families* as settlers into Perak. Lord Knutsford, Secretary of State for the Colonies, was in sympathy with the idea. Swettenham was above all keen to expand the population rapidly and was not greatly concerned about the origins of the settlers. Although some officials, notably William Edward Maxwell, did not share this free and easy approach to settlement, most state officials wholeheartedly supported the policy of encouraging settlement and agriculture by rent remissions and loans.

The colonial government had not set out specifically to create profitable opportunities for British investors. Notwithstanding its encouragement to British and other European investors the emphasis was

> *on promoting stable and permanent forms of economic activity among all sections of the community, foreign and indigenous, rather than more ephemeral ones such as pure concession hunting and land speculation. Officials on occasions effectively blocked prospective concessions to Europeans.* (Drabble, 1974, p. 202.)

Further evidence of the British administration's interest in agricultural development is found in its rice cultivation policy. Rice growing was the basis of the indigenous Malay economy, but before the British protectorate Malay rice farmers do not appear to have responded to any notable extent either to the demand of overseas markets or to that of the growing population of Chinese miners. With a growing deficiency of local production relative to local consumption of rice, the colonial government turned its attention to irrigation schemes. Drainage works were begun in Krian, in Perak, in 1890 and over 100 miles of drains were cut by 1896. Between

1898 and 1906, a comprehensive and controlled irrigation complex was constructed in Krian at a cost of $1.6 million. When completed, it irrigated 70,000 acres of land and supplied the district with potable water (Chai, 1964, pp. 99–101, 143–148).

Taken all round, government influence on development between 1874 and 1900 was considerable. The Colonial Office seemed to concur with the Residents in Malaya that the promise of future economic development justified substantial government activity and expenditure.

Private investment on the peninsula was much encouraged by the many public works and by the assured security of British governance and law. Government also created an efficient legal and administrative framework which was especially valuable to private industry. Investment was further facilitated by the introduction of a western-type system of land tenure and by regulation of the use of streams and watercourses and the disposal of tin tailings and silt. Agriculture was also encouraged by irrigation schemes and by research and experiment conducted by the Department of Agriculture established in 1905. Added to all this was official control of immigrant manpower for the export industries, coming from China, India and the Netherlands East Indies. These underpinnings of the export economy made Malaya ripe for a fortuitous export boom.

By the 1890s, a continued shortage of labour pushed government into action. The British authorities in the Straits Settlements (S.S.) and the protected Malay States were as keen for immigration as were the Chinese mine operators. Railway and road construction and other public works needed a large labour force which, without continued immigration, could only be obtained by crimping labour from the mines via higher wages and the government was so accused. In the late 1890s there arose a vicious circle of labour shortage. Immigration had been falling since 1893, while government demand for labour raised wages. The tin market suffered a temporary depression and some mining enterprises closed. The output of tin declined as, of course, did government tax revenue from tin exports. However, the price of tin surged after 1896 and labour was again scarce. "Under these circumstances the Government, with large resources at its command, was urged to import its own labour for railway construction and other public works" (Chai, 1964, p. 117).

There arose considerable agitation, by miners and other employers, for a government immigration scheme. In 1899, Swettenham as Resident-General F.M.S., introduced assistance for Chinese immigrants, for the benefit of mining employers in the Malay States. In July 1901, Swettenham (by then Governor S.S. and High Commissioner F.M.S.) drove a Bill through the Legislative Council ostensibly to protect Chinese immigrants and prevent the introduction of bubonic plague from China and Hong Kong, but also to prevent non-British ships from bringing Chinese into the colony. In 1904 a Convention was signed between the British and Chinese governments to regularise the immigration of Chinese into British colonies and protectorates. Chinese labour in the tin mining industry of the F.M.S. grew from 186,337 in 1903 to 231,368 by 1907. From 1903, the British authorities in Malaya, assisted by Christian missionary societies in China, also encouraged free Chinese immigrants as settlers and cultivators (Chai, 1964, pp. 118–123).

***

Almost co-incident with the 1896 F.M.S. was the birth of a plantation rubber industry which virtually and quickly overwhelmed previous agricultural exports. Although the feasibility of growing rubber trees in Malaya had been demonstrated in the 1880s and 1890s, large-scale commercial rubber production did not occur immediately. It was the rapid, worldwide growth of the motor-car industry after 1900 which pushed up the price of rubber to levels which made it a most profitable crop. The early years of the 20th century saw a huge increase in the demand for rubber. Between 1900 and 1910 both price and consumption of the commodity virtually doubled. In response to these circumstances, Malaya turned quickly to large-scale plantation agriculture. Investment in the development of rubber plantations was encouraged by a recession in the tin industry, which reached bottom c. 1907.

The Malayan rubber industry has been fully and extremely well chronicled in a very large literature. As well as the classic monographs by Bauer (1948), Drabble (1973) and Barlow (1978, with a bibliography of 27 pages!), there are substantial accounts of the rubber industry in the more general works by Jackson (1968), Ooi (1963) and Lim (1967) and there are countless journal articles on the subject. It is therefore needless to offer here anything more than brief reference to the rubber industry in the broader context of British enterprise in the opening up of the Malay Peninsula. The following text draws also on a more detailed account of rubber and other developments in an earlier article (Drake, 1979).

Good rubber land was available throughout Malaya. However, the rubber plantations became concentrated in the west-central and south-west regions, where an efficient transport and communications network already existed, thus facilitating the export of rubber and the import of supplies and labour (Lim, 1967, pp. 108–109). Other factors also contributed to this clustering of the plantations: the previous siting of sugar, coffee, etc. plantations in these regions; the sparse population, in the south-west particularly, which permitted the plantations to grow without encroaching on Malay farmlands; and, finally, the reformed land tenure system of the F.M.S., which made for easy alienation of land for plantations in those states.

Land for rubber was abundant but enterprise, capital and labour were needed. Some plantation enterprise and expertise were already engaged in the cultivation of coffee. Some labour was released by recession and technical change in tin mining. There were wealthy men, both Chinese and European, in the S.S. and F.M.S. who had accumulated capital from mining and trade. Since about 1850 there had been a substantial and sustained export surplus on visible trade and no direct evidence of capital import of any magnitude. After 1905, however, the rapidly expanding rubber plantation industry needed more labourers, managers and capital (Drake, 1972, pp. 951–962 deals with these input considerations).

The first rubber estates were developed by individual planters, usually those who had previously planted other crops in Malaya or Ceylon. However, when the demand for rubber expanded so rapidly after 1905, the existing individual and propriety concerns could neither finance nor organise the required increase in production. Intending planters sought the help of the British merchant firms already established in the S.S. The merchant houses applied their experience and reputations to the raising of capital and floated joint stock companies in London and Singapore. "Investors in the west were prepared to finance the expansion of the rubber industry because the companies to which they were invited to entrust their money were backed by those merchant houses known to be familiar with Malayan conditions" (Allen and Donnithorne, 1962, p. 112).

The connections between the merchant firms and the rubber companies went far beyond the mere raising of capital. The merchant houses had made themselves responsible for the commitment of enormous amounts of capital to a new industry in a region where managerial and administrative talents were scarce. The merchant firms therefore developed the agency system, which made best use of scarce talents and kept the operation of each rubber estate under the firm control of the merchant firm or, as now known, the agency house. Any agency house would supervise a number of rubber companies and an even larger number of actual plantations. A manager and staff would be appointed to organise and control production on each estate; but the broader administration, the technical and financial affairs, and the records of each company were centralised in the agency house. The staffs of the agency houses became expert in all these overhead matters because of a large scale of operations and a wide variety of experience accumulating at the control centre. Each individual rubber company therefore obtained its administrative and other overheads at a fraction of the cost at which it could have provided comparable facilities by itself. The produce of every rubber company was exported through the hands of its merchant/agency house, which also handled all imported goods used or consumed on the plantations. The merchant firms experienced a massive enlargement of their import–export trade and significant economies in finance; and by offsetting export receipts against import payments (both in foreign currency) the agency houses were often able to bypass bank credit and the foreign exchange market.

The commercial facilities provided by the British merchant firms and banks, originally established in Malayan ports to participate in the entrepot trade, were just as important to the rubber industry as the physical infrastructure originally created to serve the tin industry. In turn, the further development of commercial and physical overheads for the rubber plantations helped to stimulate smallholder rubber production by Malay peasants.

Around the turn of the century, British capital was at last moving also into the tin industry. Hitherto, mining had been carried out by Chinese, working under clan organisation and employing capital largely from wealthy Chinese in the S.S. European enterprises attempted to break into the industry with capital-intensive methods. At first they failed, not because their techniques were faulty but because they were ill-applied. The reasons for failure have been outlined colourfully by Swettenham (Allen and Donnithorne, 1962, pp. 151–152; Chai, 1964, p. 165). The Chinese saw the merits of centrifugal pumping and of the new ore-winning methods of hydraulic sluicing and gravel pumping; they adopted these innovations. "Thus the Westerners unwittingly contributed the technique which for a time confirmed their rivals' predominance" (Allen and Donnithorne, 1962, p. 152). But Western organisation and methods won in the end. The continued expansion of tin mining required deeper working, which could be done only with dredges. Tin dredges were very expensive and beyond the resources of Chinese forms of business organisation. Dredging was therefore financed by joint-stock companies in London and the Europeans began to supplant the Chinese as the principal producers of tin. In 1910, 78% of Malaya's tin production came from Chinese mines; by 1930, 63% (of a greater total) came from European-owned mines (Ooi, 1963, p. 294; Lim, 1967, pp. 51–55 and Appendix 2.1). The European mines were controlled from abroad and managed from central agencies. The methods of organisation and administration were similar to those of the rubber industry but were not conducted by the merchant houses; the management was by international mining groups which applied their expertise to the Malayan part of their worldwide operations.

It would be a mistake to interpret the evolution of international control of the mining and rubber industries as the desired outcome of conscious policies pursued by the British administration. Certainly the colonial government set about creating an environment in which private enterprise generally could flourish. But the internationalisation of the extractive industries owed essentially to the economic advantages — technical, financial, managerial and marketing — that went with large enterprises having London connections.

***

The expansion of the area under rubber trees from 50,000 acres in 1905 to 290,000 acres in 1909 (Ooi, 1963, p. 114) called for an enormous increase in the work force. The indigenous Malays were not a large population and were closely tied to their traditional agriculture and social system. It would have been interesting to see whether the Malays could have been attracted to work on the rubber estates by high wages but this seems not to have been attempted. The British managers of the estates were of the view that the Malays were resistant to forsaking their land and the ways of rural life. The rubber planters turned instead to available immigrant labour which, at the turn of the century, consisted of Indians from the declining sugar and coffee industries and Chinese released from mining by the newer capital-intensive methods.

There were also Malay-race immigrants from Java, Sumatra and elsewhere in the Netherlands East Indies. The rise in the "Malay" population in the F.M.S. from 230,090 in 1890 to 313,763 in 1900 suggests that such immigration was considerable (Chai, 1964, p. 65: Sadka, 1968, pp. 327–330, 358–360). The immigrant Malays appear to have come to take advantage of British rule, increasing prosperity and the opportunities in a relatively empty land, in which many from the East Indies already had family and other connections.

Although some 300,000 Chinese constituted the largest racial group in the F.M.S. in 1900, there were few of them to be spared for the rubber estates. Those who forsook mining generally either returned to China or engaged in trade and service occupations. Moreover, the natural increase in the Chinese labour force was insignificant because of the very small number of Chinese females in the F.M.S. and a general inability or reluctance of Chinese men to marry with other races.

In all these circumstances, the rubber planters turned to the well-known source of plantation labour — South India. The demand for Indian labour occurred at a time when there was famine and widespread unemployment in India. The Indian workers who came to Malaya were better off than if they had stayed home. It was therefore easy to recruit large numbers of Indian labourers to work in Malaya. Moreover, European employers had a preference for Indian labourers who were good and docile workers accustomed to British rule (Lim, 1967, p. 186, quoting a Malaysian historian of Indian race). Thus began the second large wave of immigration to Malaya, which reached its peak in the decade 1911–1920 and continued until World War II. Between 1881 and 1940 almost three million immigrants came to Malaya from India. Most of them eventually returned home although the permanent net migration of Indians to Malaya was still large at 750,000 persons (Ooi, 1963, p. 116).

Although there had been modest levels of Indian immigration to Penang and Singapore from the early days of British rule, the Indian government imposed restrictions at various times. The restrictions on emigration from India to the S.S. were relaxed in the 1870s but not until 1884 was Indian immigration into the Malay States legalised (Chai, 1964, p. 127).

Labourers were brought from India either under indenture to employers in Malaya or under the *kangany* method whereby planters engaged the *kangany*, who recruited men from his own village in India and received a *per capita* commission from the employer. Both methods of recruitment had fault which caused much criticism. In 1898, Governor Sir Charles Mitchell, after visiting India and conferring with Indian officials, recruiting agents and the planters, brought in and enacted a new Indian Immigration Bill and repealed all former laws on the subject. However, the new Bill did little to improve recruitment and employment practices and, despite the official aim of free immigration, a continued shortage of labour caused planters still to rely on the existing practices (Chai, 1964, pp. 127–133).

The shortage of Indian labour was exacerbated by a depreciation of the silver dollar, which made wages in Malaya less attractive than the wages in gold standard or sterling exchange countries. The S.S. government subsidised Indian recruitment by way of free or assisted sea passages from India; but on the other hand the government crimped immigrant labour from plantations into public works, causing much resentment among planters. With the price of rubber doubling between 1901 and 1905, new plantations were developed rapidly and the planters were desperate for more labour. Government sympathised and its own needs for more labour also had to be met. In 1909, Governor John Anderson introduced and eventually passed a Bill to establish a Tamil Immigration Fund, to which plantation employers were required to contribute:

The Tamil Immigration Fund was the climax of 40 years of Government legislation to regulate the flow of Indian labour into Malaya. Sir John

Anderson's brilliant idea [free passages to planters for their labour] not only solved the main problem of labour recruitment — finance — but also indirectly united the planters and prepared the way for the final formal abolition of indentured labour in 1910. By 1906 the Malay States had an estimated total of 95,000 Indians, the bulk of whom were labourers and traders. From the time the Tamil Immigration Fund came into operation, all Indian labourers were landed as free agents in Malaya, except those who were specifically recruited by private employers on the indenture system. The provision of free tickets and the fact that Malaya now [since 1904] had a currency based on gold attracted large numbers of Indian immigrants. The subsequent development of the rubber industry which was to contribute so much to stabilizing the economy of the country was due entirely to the unrestricted flow of Indian labour into Malaya. (Chai, 1964, pp. 139–140)

Although Indians dominated the early years of the second wave of immigration, this does not mean that other immigrants were unimportant. Immigration from China and the East Indies continued, and indeed the Chinese formed the principal immigrant stream in the 1920s. No accurate statistics are available of arrivals and departures of Chinese or of Malays from the East Indies. Nor is there any enumeration of the very many peninsula-born Malays who descended from Malay-race immigrants.

***

The domestic demand for foodstuffs obviously increased with growth of mining, plantations and urban populations and the production of foodstuffs for sale was cheapened by the improvements in communications and transport. Some Malays — indigenous and immigrant — did undertake the production of foodstuffs for sale but, in general, the Malays did not appear to expand their agricultural output either for export or to sell to the growing population of Chinese and Indians. The British administration encouraged the Malays to develop their agricultural smallholdings: for example, by the dissemination of improved rice seed, better implements, irrigation and by spreading knowledge of cropping and marketing. Considerable assistance was also given by way of finance. A central government loan fund for agricultural development was established in 1908, and long before then small loans to farmers had been distributed through village officials.

It is patently untrue that the colonial administrators kept the Malays tied to rice cultivation and denied them opportunities for growing other, wholly commercial crops. As a cash crop, rice was neither very profitable for the farmer nor a good source of revenue for the government; this was reflected in the fact that traditional rice lands were not uncommonly given over, without restriction, to other cash crops. At the same time, the administrators were concerned to maintain rice production by the Malays because it was their traditional activity and staple food, and free of any distress which might result from dependence on variable markets, to the exclusion of agriculture for subsistence (Sadka, 1968, p. 355–356).

There is little evidence of Malay response to official encouragement to commercial agriculture before the turn of the century. From the 1880s some Malays had engaged in cash cropping of coffee; during the 1890s some smallholders in Perak planted rubber trees but they must have been few in number because total rubber acreage was very small until after 1905. However, "from 1910 onwards, there was a rush by Malay smallholders to grow the crop. In some cases they cut down their fruit trees and even planted their padi fields with rubber" (Ooi, 1963, p. 202). The area of smallholdings under rubber increased rapidly; by 1922 smallholdings totalling 918,000 acres accounted for 40% of the total acreage under rubber (Lim, 1967, p. 105). The ready availability of land was one factor encouraging the rapid expansion of rubber production by indigenous and immigrant Malays alike. The other important supply factors were the simplicity of techniques, the limited capital equipment needed, and the unique labour demands of the rubber tree which could be met from within the farmer's family. It was not a matter of substituting rubber for rice or other food crops. Rubber production could be started as a supplement to padi cultivation. Indeed, a source of subsistence was needed during the half-dozen years of waiting for a rubber tree to yield latex. When the trees did begin to yield, the crop had the advantage of a non-seasonal flow of latex and so the labour of tapping could be performed at times which did not clash with the labour demands of the padi crop. Rubber production could be done in a manner which was initially riskless to the peasant farmer's livelihood. Moreover, rubber production did not necessarily require any great change to the Malay social system; it could be carried out on existing landholdings and without any break-up of the family unit. The fact that rubber production could be absorbed so easily into the existing way of life goes a long way towards explaining why rubber was the crop which did pull the Malays into the market economy.

***

The tin discoveries around 1850 brought Chinese entrepreneurs and labourers and British government to the Malay peninsula, and at the same time contributed business growth for Chinese and British traders at the S.S. ports. The location of the tin mines determined both the distribution of Chinese immigrants and the pattern of railways and towns. The railways and other social capital were created by a development-minded British administration and financed by revenue from tin exports. In due course, the location of social capital and population determined the siting of the plantation rubber industry. The rubber industry was greatly aided by the British administration which directly fostered labour immigration and indirectly encouraged foreign investment. As the rubber industry thrived it induced further growth of social capital and overhead facilities, physical and commercial. The development of these facilities in order to serve the processing, transport, marketing and supplies needs of the plantations also lowered the cost of producing rubber by smallholders. This lower cost plus the demonstration that rubber cultivation was easily adaptable to smallholdings drew the Malays, native and immigrant, into commercial export production.

***

The rapid development of large rubber plantations required not only immigrant labour but also imports of consumer goods for the managers, labourers and other workers on the estates. The rubber estates industry also needed imports of capital goods, suitable land for expansion, transportation services to the Straits ports, shipping capacity to Europe, familiarity with European markets for the sale of rubber and the purchase of supplies and as a means of raising, rapidly, large sums of capital for financing all these aspects of the new rubber industry.

The merchant firms were uniquely placed to assist in fulfilling all these needs. They already had marketing and financing knowledge and strong connections in Britain, and had shipping and insurance experience and agencies. Above all, perhaps, their long-proven good names in London commercial circles provided the necessary reassurance for the British public to subscribe substantial sums to new rubber-producing companies floated with their assistance. The merchants did indeed seize the opportunities provided by the rubber boom and became deeply involved in the establishment and subsequent development of the plantation rubber industry. Not surprisingly, this move had far-reaching effects on the nature and content of their hitherto import–export business. The character of the merchants changed considerably over some 15 years, so that by 1920 they were more accurately described as agency houses. Indeed by 1911, six leading European firms held a total of 365 agencies comprising 286 in the fields of insurance, shipping, banking, imported goods and a further 79 managing agencies for export producers and government (Chiang, 1970, p. 254; Drabble and Drake, 1981, p. 307. The text that follows draws very much from the latter article).

The changing activities of the firms were associated with structural changes in the merchant/agency field, taking the form of incorporations and amalgamations. That the firms sought limited liability corporate status was natural in view of the large financial risks which they were suddenly called upon to assume on behalf of embryonic rubber companies. It seems obvious, too, that the suddenly expanding scale of business in the early 20th century, and its continuing competitive nature, would provoke rationalisation through the amalgamation of firms with complementary interests. The Borneo Co. Limited had been incorporated in London as early as 1856 but it was the exception. The other firms were not incorporated until the late 19th or early 20th century. Harrisons & Crosfield took corporate status in 1908, Guthrie and Co. Limited in 1903. Paterson, Simons Co. Limited was incorporated in 1907, following the amalgamation of Paterson, Simons & Co. with Wm McKerrow & Co. Adamson, Gilfillan and Co. Limited was incorporated in 1904, by merger of Gilfillan Wood & Co. with Adamson, Gilfillan & Co. A.C. Harper and Co. Limited was incorporated in 1916, merging the unincorporated firms of A.C. Harper & Co. and J. & Q. McClymont and Co. Subsequently, in 1930 and

1935 these two groups amalgamated finally as Harper, Gilfillan and Co. Limited.

The first notable change in the business of the firms was a general loss of interest in exporting Straits produce such as copra, gambier and hides. Although a few firms remained as produce specialists and even Bousteads continued to maintain a large business in produce, the produce business of most firms declined relatively if not absolutely. Indeed Guthries closed its London produce department in 1910. New agency houses emerged which had no past connections with produce exports or with importing. The most notable of these was Sime Darby and Co. which arose in 1902 from the merger of various planter interests (Allen and Donnithorne, 1962, p. 57). Harrisons & Barker Limited (from 1921 the Malayan subsidiary of Harrisons & Crosfield Ltd., London) whose import trade previously had been relatively small (because such profitable lines as spirits, tobacco etc. had been repugnant to the firm and proscribed in its articles of association by its Quaker founders) but which had experience of plantation management in Ceylon, grew quickly to become one of the major agency houses in Malaya. T. Barlow and Brothers, originally importers of Manchester goods but without any export trade in produce, quickly established itself as a leading agency for rubber companies.

There was also a very considerable growth, and shift in the internal composition, of the import trade. The development of the rubber plantations gave rise to demand for the import of capital goods, such as machinery and engineering items, and estate supplies; so the traditional consumer imports of cottons, woollens, spirits and opium diminished in importance. It should be noted too that estate imports, both capital and consumer lines, were related to the state and prospects of rubber exports. Any general decline in export activity raised the danger of the merchants being overstocked on imports, a cause of frequent concern to Guthrie & Co. and illustrated in correspondence between their Singapore and London offices in 1918–1920, for example.

The capital-raising activities of the mercantile firms or agency houses gave them intimate connections with the newly-floated rubber companies and led naturally to continuing secretarial, and often managerial, roles for those companies (Drabble, 1973, pp. 78–86). The management and administration of the rubber plantation companies often became a dominant aspect of agency house work. It must further be recognised that an agency house, or its proprietors, usually held some shares in each of the various plantation companies under its management. In descending order of involvement, an agency house could be owner, major shareholder, minority shareholder, contract manager and/or secretary to any given rubber-producing company. Any substantial equity in the company naturally drew the agency house into managerial and secretarial functions, although agency houses sometimes performed merely secretarial roles for companies in which they held no shares. Any managerial/secretarial connection with a rubber company — often no more than a seat on the board of directors without shareholding — brought lucrative selling and supplying agencies and commissions to the agency houses.

The management and merchant activities were not invariably intertwined. Some firms specialised in one or other type of activity: for example, McAlister and Co. remained merchants pure and simple, whereas Cumberbatch and Co. (a firm which incidentally had come over from Ceylon) and the Rubber Estate Agency of London confined themselves to managing agency and secretarial roles, as did Harrisons & Crosfield, which was not a merchant firm in Malaya like Guthries and Bousteads, but an agency house there from 1903 when it first invested in rubber plantations. By 1914, Harrisons & Crosfield had established, and acted as agents for, a large number of rubber plantations.

Those large houses (such as Guthries, Harrisons & Crosfield, Bousteads) which were much involved in estate management maintained "Estates" departments in which staff specialised in various aspects of rubber estate management and administration, applying their knowledge across several estates. The European staff on any estate were few in number and they drew on the agency house in Singapore or Kuala Lumpur for a vast number of services. Thus the agency house maintained staffs of agriculturalists, engineers and accountants who travelled from estate to estate, both on regular visits and as particular needs arose. Technically and economically, this was a most efficient system: economies of scale were reaped in the employment of professionals whose skills were extended and sharpened by a wide range of comparative experience on different estates in various parts of Malaya. The agency houses also trained and maintained a pool of estate managers; the usual practice was to bring young men out from Britain and send them around various estates as assistants before eventually making them managers (Wright and Cartwright, 1908, pp. 381–494). Staff were a large and constant worry for the agency houses, both their own staff and the estates staff (this is a large and rich story of which the following chapter gives some illustrations; its social aspects have long attracted novelists, notably W. Somerset Maugham). Suffice it now to remark that, worry notwithstanding, the staff were on the whole capable and appear in general to have served long contracts; many made lifetime careers in Malaya.

The intricate, and sometimes tangled, involvement of the agency houses as managers/secretaries to plantation companies which were separate entities, in law at least, gave rise to a good deal of ambiguity about roles, created diffused responsibilities, and caused conflicts of interest. These difficulties are best exemplified in the disagreements which often erupted between the rubber companies and their managing agents on two similar issues: the scale of fees charged for managerial/secretarial work, and the commissions exacted by the agents on supplies imported for the estates. Guthries records bear well on these issues. In 1917 we find their Singapore manager complaining to London that estate management *per se* was unremunerative at the then level of fees and that in consequence the staff in the Estates department tended to become disheartened. He argued that the fact that the firm profited otherwise by its estate connections — principally by commission on the sale of rubber — was irrelevant. These other rewards were justly earned for the relevant services and their existence "constitutes no good reason why the companies should not pay proper fees for the agency services rendered" (Guthrie letters, Singapore to London, 6 September 1917).

A few years earlier, Guthries had been sued by a constituent company, Bukit Kajang Rubber Estates Limited, for damages in breach of the management agreement, on the grounds that Guthries made a profit on goods supplied to the estate. The "profit" was never denied but Guthries alleged that that Bukit Kajang had also violated the agreement by not purchasing all their supplies through Guthries. The Singapore manager of Guthries went on to claim that the agreement had been badly drafted and that it was never Guthrie's intention to waive profits on estate supplies and be content with a mere 2½% handling commission.

Whenever there was any sustained or heavy fall in rubber prices the agency houses found their estate connections onerous and worrying. This was principally because, unless the estate companies had considerable liquid reserves, the agency houses were called upon to make advances of working capital to tide the estates over periods of lean revenue; whereas if the agents declined to advance they risked the future loss of the "extremely profitable" rubber selling business from the estate (Guthrie letters, Singapore to London, 20 June 1918).

By the early 1920s the agency houses clearly held the whip hand. The rubber plantation companies that then constituted the industry were generally too small individually to ride out price fluctuations, to maintain technical and managerial expertise, and to foster agricultural research and development. All of these needs, however, could be met under the protective umbrella of the agency houses which, in that period, built up their respective groups of client estate, and in some cases mining, companies.

Chapter 7

Merchant Firm 1: Guthrie & Co.

In Chapter 1, the origins and activities of merchant firms were described in a general way. This chapter and the next one deal in detail with two of the largest and most prominent firms, drawing mainly on private letter books to tell of the firms' operations, concerns and personalities. The present chapter deals with Guthrie & Co. and the following one with Boustead & Co.

The rubber plantations boom led the firms away from being traders pure and simple to embrace also the lucrative business of managing agents for plantation enterprises. However, the firms were essentially unchanged in ownership, style and philosophy. Until the early 20th century, the businesses remained merchant firms trading in imports to and exports from Singapore, Malaya and Borneo. However, once the rubber plantation industry became ascendant, the business of the firms shifted towards the agency services of providing supplies, staff, administration and accounting to the rubber plantations, and the selling of their rubber output. Then the term "agency houses" emerged. Nevertheless, the business of exporting other produce items did not decline in absolute terms. Indeed, Boustead & Co. remained a very strong exporter of traditional produce, whereas Guthrie & Co. moved rather more into agency work for the rubber industry but did not abandon other produce.

***

121

Guthrie and Co. Ltd. was incorporated and registered in Singapore on 28 February 1903 with a nominal capital of $1 million. The company then branched into Penang in 1905 and Kuala Lumpur in 1910, although unincorporated forms of the firm and partnerships had previously existed in those places. The antecedents of Guthrie & Co. Ltd. were much earlier, as described in Chapter 1, its immediate predecessor being the unincorporated Guthrie and Co. from 1833. A detailed and colourful history of the firm in its various forms has been published and is recommended (Cunyngham-Brown, 1971). That volume deals mainly with personalities and politics in a broad sense; the present chapter looks more closely at the internal operations and concerns of Guthries in the late 19th and early 20th centuries, when it broadened from a trading firm to become also an agency house.

The predominant concerns over this period were of a financial nature, especially the constant tension between the Singapore and London offices about the division of cash reserves and the workload, with each side claiming oppression by the other. In 1913, A.E. Baddeley in Singapore wrote a scorcher of a letter to London in the following terms:

> *It seems to us that the main object in view in London is to make work for us out here and to carp and criticize without justification. Extra work means time, yours, ours and the Estate staff's, and time is money which someone must pay — either we or the Company.... The tendency to throw more and more detail work on us is to be deprecated, especially if it is work that can be done by you in London as European clerical assistance costs much more here than in London ... the fees allowed for us as Eastern Agents are far from adequate remuneration for the services rendered.* (Baddeley, Singapore to London, 24 April 1913.)

In 1901, A.J. Ross of Guthrie & Co., as agents for Scott & Co. (London), became especially worried about the growing size of drafts being drawn on C.S. Seng & Co. of Penang. Seng's accumulated acceptances amounted to the very large sum of £4,000, when the exchange rate was about 2 shillings to 1 Straits dollar. Guthries therefore sought supporting guarantees from Seng's partners, notably Cheah Choon Sen. Notwithstanding this concern, Guthries continued to do business with Seng & Co. and solicited Seng's quotation for handling, on behalf of Guthries, kerosene oil on offer from the Standard Oil Co. of New York (Ross, Letter Book, 22 March, 13 August 1901). In the same year, Ross wrote (24 July) to the Raja Muda of Kedah indicating that the Kedah government was indebted at least $4,000 to Guthries for goods and cash advances. He wrote (31 August) to W. Wingrove & Co. of London, giving a poor credit opinion of M.C.S. Mohamed & Co., jewellers of Singapore, and complaining also of Mohamed's attempt to bypass Guthries by ordering goods direct from London. Other Ross correspondence indicates that Guthries were interested at the time in pearls, sandalwood, fire clay, roll zinc and tin plate.

Ross became dissatisfied and resigned from Guthries at the end of the year. He took a position in Fremantle working with Shrager Bros. John Anderson responded to this move by an action against Ross for breach of agreement in working for Shragers within three years of leaving Guthries. Anderson was bad-tempered and vengeful because, through Ross, Shragers got a foothold in the pearl and sandalwood export trades (Letter Books of Fremantle, 1902–1906).

Guthries own business in Fremantle appeared not to flourish. Its general import trade fell by two-thirds between December 1901 and March 1903 (Singapore to Fremantle, 22 July 1903), and its expenditures of about £9,000 per annum were regarded as high in relation its average annual turnover of £110,000, i.e. almost 9% of turnover. "In Singapore, we might point out by way of contrast, the turnover — exclusive of tin — is quite £100,000 per month and the expenses a trifle under £10,000 per annum — a proportion of less than 1% of the turnover" (Anderson, Singapore, to F.W. Barrymore, Fremantle, 22 July 1903). Subsequently, Anderson needed to soothe Barrymore after at first intending to send Duncan Paterson into the manager position in Fremantle (Anderson to Barrymore, 15 August 1903 and 22 July 1905).

Around this time, Guthries were interested in the Sunghie Ayam Mining Concession in Kemaman which was held by an important native Chinese, Tham Kay Chiang. The concession to Tham had been granted by Sultan Zainalabidin of Trengganu, for 60 years from 11 July 1896, for exclusive mining and other rights, including planting, over approximately 50 square miles at Kemaman for a royalty of 10% of whatever was exported. This was stated to be the customary rate of royalty on tin mined in the unprotected Malay states, whereas in the protected states of Perak and Selangor the rate was "considerably higher" because of the benefits of roads and railways available in those states. It was concluded that the concessional property was very rich in tin and potentially of great value; the disadvantages of getting stores and machinery up to the mines, and of importing Chinese labourers, were regarded as mere inconveniences (Report to Messrs Guthrie & Co., Singapore by Mr George Laws M.E.; A.I.M.M. dated 20 April 1902).

In the same year, John Anderson of Guthries applied for five 50-acre blocks of gold-bearing land in the neighbourhood of Batu Bersawah. It was stated that Thomas Scott of Singapore and Captain Lawson were equally interested on the basis of one-third each (C. Macdonald, Acting District Officer, Land Office, Kwala Pilah, September 1902).

From sundry letters and statements prepared by A. Hood-Begg of the import department of Guthries in Penang, the difficulties of agency houses between 1906 and 1909 are revealed. The Penang business of Guthries was mostly imports of piece goods and rough goods such as "Elephant" undershirts and "Hennesseys" brandy. Exports from Penang were tin ore, hides and other produce. According to the recollections of Baddeley, who served with Guthries from 1898 to 1921, the produce business, even including tin ore, was never very profitable, "the backbone of the Firm's business was undoubtedly imports — both rough goods and piece goods". The years 1907–1908 were particularly bad for Penang's trade. The import market was dull and many traders were caught with excess stocks, especially of tin ore which had been bought speculatively. In that year there were many failures and all the European agency firms were caught with bad debts. Hood-Begg prepared a list of 19 firms with debt losses of $391,103 from 1 July 1907 to 30 June 1908, and a further $84,761 for the month of July 1908 (Hood-Begg to Anderson, 14 October 1908). Guthries came in fifth place while their great rival Bousteads topped the list.

As early as the 1890s, Guthrie connections were acquiring land on the peninsula. In 1895 the Linggi Liberian Coffee Co. Ltd. was purchased for $4,000 from a London vendor by three parties including Charles Malcolm Cumming, a relative of the Guthrie family. Linggi acquired 1,000 acres of vacant jungle land in Sungei Ujong, Negri Sembilan. Cumming was appointed Resident Manager of the estate for 12 years from 1 November 1895 on generous terms. In 1905 the company changed its name to Linggi

Plantations Ltd. and purchased the nearby Ulu Sawah estate. The purpose of these transactions, and the subsequent purchase of Kanchong Estate, was to undertake rubber planting with which Cumming had been experimenting since 1896. Guthries were the agents for the company and R.F. McNair Scott, the London director of Guthries, joined the Linggi board. Linggi Plantations acquired land in Selangor and the Kamuning Estate in Perak in 1908. Then it bought the neighbouring Heawood Estate in 1909. The last transaction involved a bitter battle between the Scott and Anderson interests, in which the latter was victorious; a casualty in this event was Baddeley who Scott and Cumming had appointed to be Chairman of the board of directors of their Elphinstone Estates vehicle which sought to acquire Heawood (Cunyngham-Brown, 1971, pp. 184, 230–231).

In the first decade of the 20th century, there was a rush by British and European firms to obtain land grants, especially for the nascent rubber plantation industry:

> *A heavy and continuous demand for land followed from 1902 to 1906, only to be checked by the action of the Government in introducing high premiums and quit rents. There was a further check due to an insufficient flow of labour for the upkeep and further development of already acquired land, now remedied, however, by new labour regulations. As it was, the area under rubber passed from 7,500 acres in 1902 to 180,000 in 1907. (Straits Times, 6 January 1909.)*

As one example, an agreement was made on 14 December 1904 between Guthrie & Co. Ltd. of Singapore and Thomas Heslop Hill of Seremban, by which the company purchased from T.H. Hill, for $79,811, a half-share in four properties: Bukit Nanas Estate in Seremban of 324 acres; Negri Sembilan Rubber Estate in Seremban of 726 acres; Klang Lands Estate in Klang of 1,518 acres; Haron Estate in Klang of 430 acres. These properties mostly grew rubber and coffee in various degrees. Thus was formed the Bukit Nanas Syndicate as a joint venture between Guthries and Hill. It was agreed that reasonable working capital would be advanced as necessary by Guthries and the company would be entitled to interest at 5% p.a. on such advances until repaid. Guthries and Hill would share equally the profits and losses of the Syndicate. The company would manage the

Syndicate and enjoy the right to sell all produce from the properties and be entitled to a commission of 2% on the gross price of all such sales. Further, Guthrie & Co. were authorised to sell or float any or all of the properties of the Syndicate, provided that "any commissions paid to the Managers on the sale of any of the said properties shall be treated as part of the assets of the Syndicate" (Agreement between Guthries and Hill made at Singapore, 14 December 1904).

Fragmentary records survive of Guthries Penang business in tin and produce. From March 1906 to August 1908, Guthries earned £5,103 (= $43,746 @ 2s.4d) on the export of 7,980 tons of tin sold in London on behalf of 13 Chinese firms. In August 1908, Guthries purchased 150 tons of tin (from Straits Trading, Eastern Smelting and Chin Guan) for a total of $177,400, to meet London orders of 200 tons for about £815; they thus oversold 50 tons temporarily. In produce, Guthries spent $48,400 buying pepper, tapioca, buffalo hides and patchouli leaves from various Chinese produce dealers, and held produce stocks valued at $38,842 as at 10 August 1908 (lists prepared by S.E. Amsberg in the Penang office and given to A. Hood-Begg on 12 August 1908).

Guthries did a continual business of money-lending in Singapore. A regular borrower was R.M.C.A.L. Alagappah Chitty, who was an associate of the Chinese headman Loke Yew. In 1901, he borrowed $35,000 on 19 mortgages to Scott and Anderson, which he duly paid off; in 1903 and 1907 he borrowed on the security of his shares in the Raub Australian Gold Mining Co. Ltd. which were lodged with Guthries. It is evident that Alagappah Chitty was associated with Guthries and Loke Yew in several ventures:

— Chitty had a one-tenth share of Guthrie's 50% of the profits and losses of the Kamuning Estate.
— Chitty had a one-tenth share in Loke Yew's mining on Kamuning.
— When the Kamuning Estate was sold to Linggi Plantations Ltd. in 1908, Chitty received $43,875 net for his one-tenth share of Guthries half-ownership. He subsequently held shares in and received dividends from Linggi Plantations.
— Chitty had a twelve-nineteenths share in the Perak General Farm, which yielded him $18,080 over 1903–1905 (Receipt and Release by

Administrators of the late R.M.C.A.L. Alagappah Chitty in favour of Guthrie & Co., dated 17 May 1912).

Among the minor debtors to Guthries were: Ismail, $3,000 on an on-demand promissory note dated 14 October 1903; S. Tomlinson on an unsecured I.O.U. dated 17 November 1915 until 17 March 1916, and Tomlinson was charged interest at 8% p.a. on this accommodation.

Guthries maintained a substantial Register of shares, investments and deeds held by the company on behalf of the partners, staff and clients. The following share lodgings are notable.

THOMAS SCOTT: Sayle & Co., Straits Insurance, Tanjong Pagar Dock, Straits Fire Insurance, National Marine Insurance, Bundi Tin Mining, Raub Australia Gold Mining, Malay Peninsula Coffee Co. Ltd., Pahang Corporation Ltd., Pahang Kabang Ltd., Bersawah Gold Mining Co. Ltd., The Straits Trading Co. Ltd.

JOHN ANDERSON: Singapore Cold Storage Co. Ltd., Pahang Corporaton Ltd., Raub Australia Gold Mining, Bundi Tin Mining, Malay Peninsula Coffee Co. Ltd., Bersawah Gold Mining Co. Ltd., Tanjong Pagar Dock, Pahang Kabang Ltd., Jelebu Mining and Trading Co. Ltd., and many rubber estate companies.

H.H. SULTAN IDRIS MARSIDAL AAZAM SHAH of PERAK: Raub Australia Gold Mining.

R.P.A. SWETTENHAM: Raub Australia Gold Mining.

W.H. TREACHER: Singapore Insurance Co. Ltd., Sayle & Co., Borneo Hotel and Stores Co., China Borneo Co. Ltd., also mortgages by Rudolph & Jose Luis 'Cotta $1,800 and Gan Eng Seng $3,000 (letter in Investment Register, p. 226).

JAMES GUTHRIE DAVIDSON: Rawang Tin, Tanjong Pagar Dock. At his death at the end of 1905, Davidson held the following assets in the hands of Guthries: mortgages over property in Battery Road and Boat Quay amounting to $132,233 @ 7% p.a.; money "lying in our hands" of $121,023 @ 4% p.a. interest. The annual interest on these sums amounted to $14,097. Davidson also left a share of 44.1446% in the Trafalgar Estate (loose memorandum dated 3 January 1906 in the Investment Register).

Wm. J. COATES of Batu Labu Estate lodged share certificates, land leases and land grants with Guthries in 1899, 1903, 1905 "as security for advances that may be made against coffee crop". Further advances in 1906, 1907, 1908 were made but no longer specifically against coffee crops, implying that the estate had moved into rubber planting.

Guthries lent money on many mortgages over property in Singapore between 1881 and 1903 executed mostly by Singapore Chinese, and also several Malays, Chittys and Europeans, in favour of Scott, Anderson and their legal associate Bernard Rodyk. Interest rates on the surviving documents range from 7% to 12%, so the business was very profitable. In April–May 1887, for example, 12 short-term loans, all but one to Chinese, were made totalling $61,500 @ 8% p.a. The loan funds were provided by Guthrie & Co. and their clients, including the Estate of Gan Eng Seng, Dr T.J. Rowell, Estate of Sophia C. Guthrie, R.F.McN. Scott and Sir William Hood Treacher. Large mortgage loans were often broken down among several creditors. A table survives of "Declarations re monies invested on Mortgage" from 31 December 1900 to 17 January 1911, amounting to a total of almost $1.5 million.

Anderson, Scott, Catchick Paul Chater and Chia Ah Cham were active in the formation of the Bundi Tin Mining Syndicate in 1899 and its subsequent workings up to 1910. The original land concession dated 3 September 1889 was given by H.H. Sultan Jemal Abidin bin Sultan Almarhome of Tringanu to Chia Ah Cham.

A further significant concession was given by H.H. The Sultan of Johore (Ibrahim) to Sir Frank Swettenham re The Rubber Estates of Johore Ltd. (Deed of Concession, 14 November 1905). Subsequently, H.H. The Sultan undertook to make grants to The Rubber Estates of Johore Ltd. in accordance with the share concession to Sir Frank Swettenham (Approval of Selection, 18 June 1908). Swettenham was feathering his retirement nest on the basis of his longstanding connections and influence all over British Malaya, as doubtless were other British administrators of the period.

Another string to Guthrie's bow of influence was an arrangement with the Colonial Secretary for the purchase of opium on behalf of the governments of the Straits Settlements (S.S.) and the Federated Malay States

(F.M.S.) (Agreement dated 5 October 1909). Similarly, Guthries negotiated an agreement whereby all the opium required by the North Borneo
Opium and Spirit monopolies was to be provided by Guthries. However,
Guthries complained that their sole right to buy opium for Borneo was
breached by Chee Swee Cheng (Baddeley to Government Secretary,
Jesselton, 6 June 1913). The profitability of opium was illustrated in the
case of requirements for the Bundi Tin Mines at Kemaman where *chandu*
costing $2,415, together with duty and charges of $290, would yield the
Chinese retailer — Leong Guan — a gross profit of $8,005 (Hood-Begg
to F.J. Martin, Bundi Tin Mines, 24 June 1913).

Considerable correspondence between Singapore and London later
in 1913 indicates the importance to Guthries of the coaling of ships in
Singapore. There was fear expressed that Lim Chin Tsong of Rangoon
might be made bankrupt, thus ruining Guthrie's very profitable business of coaling his steam ships at Singapore. Guthries were under
contract to purchase Japanese coal and relied mainly on Lim's steamers
to absorb it. Practically every week, Guthries drafts on him were falling due in Rangoon. The drafts were met promptly, the steamers ran
regularly, and no complaints were evident of any delays in payments
for salaries, wages, provisions and other expenditure in connection
with running the steamers. At any one time, outstanding drafts were
$20,000–$30,000 in value. So Guthrie's concern about Lim's survival
was ill-founded (Singapore to London, 28 August and 10 September
1913).

The Singapore Municipality Loan of 1913 was undersubscribed and
so Guthries, acting with and for Singapore Electric Tramways, proposed
terms to take up the balance. The Electric Tramways Company was motivated by a desire to see the electricity system of the municipality extended.
Guthries Singapore suggested to London that the Chartered Bank might
also co-operate in taking up the balance of the loan floatation (Singapore
to London, 17, 25 February and 18 March 1914).

In 1914, Bukit Kajang Rubber Estates Ltd. sued Guthries for damages in breach of an agreement and for rescission of the agreement on
account of the breach. The alleged breach was that Guthries made a profit
on goods supplied to the estate. However, Singapore claimed that Bukit

Kajang violated another clause in the agreement by not channelling all their purchases through Guthries. For purchasing goods for companies they represented, Guthries charged a flat 2½% but in addition billed the companies for incidental expenses, sometimes inflated:

> *Any of the other companies with whom we have agreements may revisit the point as to whether any other profit than the 2½% allowed under the agreement on all the goods supplied to them. And, if this point should be raised, we should have on our hands half a dozen or more cases more or less identical with that of Bukit Kajang.* (Hood-Begg, Singapore, to Anderson, London, 27 February 1914.)

Hood-Begg therefore proposed to settle quickly and quietly with Bukit Kajang.

A month later, Hood-Begg wrote to Anderson in critical and intemperate terms about a proposal for Guthries to amalgamate with Sime Darby & Co. This proposal was put forward by Guthrie employees W.H. Sime and J.S.M. Rennie, both formerly of Sime Darby. They argued that amalgamation would add to the number of company agencies and the volume of rubber sales in Singapore. Hood-Begg was pessimistic about the future of Singapore as a rubber market and felt also that company secretaryships were not profitable business. Within Guthries, Singapore, both Baddeley and Jno. Robertson disagreed with Hood-Begg, arguing that Singapore would develop into a major market for first-class rubber and that taking over the estates run by Sime Darby & Co. would be a profitable line. It seems that Baddeley and Robertson were the better judges (Hood-Begg, Singapore, to Anderson, London, 10 March 1914).

Financial tensions between London and Singapore — always present — flared up again in late 1917. Robertson rebuked London because, over a long time, sterling pounds revenue from Singapore exports exceeded the sterling value of Singapore's imports and London held on to the balance:

> *The monies collected and retained by you over a long period have been considerably in excess of the value of "free" shipments sent to us ... the volume of such shipments has fallen off while the estate requisitions have mounted up and it was only because profits here were in many*

cases exceptional while stocks of produce were running down to a low level that we were able to carry on for so long without calling upon you ... at the end of July we found it necessary to hold a considerable quantity of Tin (this indeed appears to be a constant factor now) while we have also had to replenish our stocks of Produce. Next month we shall have some heavy outgoings and, although we shall certainly not call upon you without good reason, it is possible we may find it necessary to ask you for a remittance. (Robertson, Singapore to London, 20 September 1917.)

The upshot of this letter was a telegraphic transfer from London of £20,000, through the Chartered Bank, which was placed on fixed deposit for three months at 3% p.a.

Trade in Singapore was also hindered at this time by an external drain of silver coin for melting, consequent on a rise in the price of silver. This was of concern to Guthrie & Co. The Straits government had suspended encashment of dollar notes for coin, and was issuing small denomination notes, even as low as 10 cents, to make up for the currency circulation shortage caused by the export of silver coin, "much of the smaller coinage having been sent away before Government really tumbled to the game" (Robertson, Singapore to London, 2 November 1917).

In early 1918, government restrictions on rubber production caused a drop in exports and in import turnover. Moreover, at the same time as this trade decline Guthries experienced

so much competition from Japanese traders that we are reluctantly compelled to look for a further falling off in our turnover ... the influx of Japanese into Singapore has been tremendous. Many of them have set up as small traders and estate supplies form a line which practically all of them are endeavouring to handle. Under the circumstances, we fear that competition is bound to become ruinously keen. (Robertson, Singapore to London, 25 February 1918.)

For example, Japanese undershirts were sent to Java where they were stamped and labelled with Guthries "Elephant" brand by a Chinese firm. The stamp and labels were evidently supplied from Japan. The label was "a perfect copy" of Guthrie's original label (Robertson, Singapore to London, 14 March 1918).

Then emerged a drying up of produce supplies from the Dutch East Indies to Singapore, as the Japanese were doing extensive direct business from Java to Japan (Robertson, Singapore to London, 10 May 1918). Worse, there was a heavy fall in the price of rubber, barely covering the cost of production. Small producers, who supplied much rubber to Guthries, were in particular difficulty and, as they lacked cash reserves, Guthries feared a demand by producers for loan funds.

> *This rubber selling business has been extremely profitable and it is only natural that, in the event of our declining assistance when it is asked for, the rubber selling of the estates which we may have to turn down will afterwards be placed in the hands of firms who are prepared to render help in the present difficult times.* (Robertson, Singapore to London, 20 June 1918.)

As rubber estates loomed larger in Guthrie's business they raised also the contentious matter of agency fees. Guthries took the view that agency work required experienced and capable men, who did not come cheaply. So low rates of commission made the activity barely remunerative to the firm and disheartening to staff in the Estates Department, despite the fact that Guthries profited from the ancillary commissions on rubber sales. Baddeley wrote at length to London about the inadequacy of agency fees (Baddeley, Singapore, to London, 6 September 1917). London agreed that that rubber estate agency fees were inadequate but hoped that better times would be available when the industry recovered from the current depression. Baddeley pointed out that the Estates Department in Singapore comprised three Europeans (one of doubtful competence) to conduct the agency work and do the estates accounts. This was insufficient but the low agency fees could not support an increase in staff:

> *Are we to have an estates department staff here which costs more than it earns, in the hope that within a reasonable time our remuneration will be put on an adequate footing, or, that it is justifiable on the ground that it enables the firm to make substantial profits in other ways — such as rubber selling in London, supply of estate requirements and engineering material?* (Baddeley, Singapore, to London, 21 November 1918.)

Baddeley did not share the opinion that estate work could be done by Chinese, Eurasian or Tamil clerks under the supervision of one or two Europeans. After describing the many activities and difficulties of estate work, he believed that there should be three or four European men doing estate management and another competent one on estate accounts. He also felt that Singapore should be in closer touch with estates because "the absence of close touch with estates multiplies correspondence, weakens our own grip on control over estates and of course impairs our close knowledge of details of the estate working." He further suggested that transfer of the Estates Department to Kuala Lumpur should be considered (Baddeley, Singapore, to London, 21 November 1918).

A related matter to the estates was whether or not it was desirable for Guthries staff in Singapore to sit as directors on the boards of local companies. London raised the question of time lost to Guthries, though admitting that it was sometimes necessary to have men on boards to protect Guthries interests. Baddeley maintained that seats on boards were very advantageous to Guthries:

> *In every case here a seat on the Board carries with it, as a condition, the selling of estate rubber and there is a considerable danger that resignation from the Board will mean the passing of the rubber selling to a rival firm,* [as had happened with the Changkat Salak and Heawood companies,] *it would be a very great pity to throw away ... selling agencies which we now hold by reason of our having a representative on the Boards and without the firm having had to invest any of its money in the companies concerned ... not only are these connections directly profitable in themselves but they lead to other things — to business in estate supplies, machinery and insurance and to new connections with other rubber producers.* (Baddeley, Singapore, to London, 2 August 1919.)

Fair comment, but one wonders if Baddeley was thinking also of his own fees as a director of such companies?

Singapore trade was dull after the World War I Armistice. Locals expected import prices to fall, as was justified by some large holdings of stocks by merchant firms. Nor was there optimism about the Singapore export trade, which to some extent had been lost during the War, while fresh competition locally was feared from the Japanese and the Dutch. It was therefore regretted by Guthries that the firm had so few local standbys to provide revenue in bad times. Robertson drew a comparison between the deep involvement of British merchant firms in industrial undertakings in India and China and the lack of comparable interest in the S.S. Consequently, local industries appeared to fall more and more into the hands of Chinese such as Lim Peng Siang. "There may be industries which it pay us to develop and we commend the matter to your consideration" (Robertson, Singapore, to London, 29 November 1918).

In early August 1919, Singapore was concerned about the size of its local bank overdraft which was fluctuating between $1 million and $1.8 million. Baddeley thought it unlikely that Singapore's financial position would be continuously and permanently reduced by the gradual, slow accumulation of profits locally. Good profits made in the last few years "have been used in buying out the Scott interest, in paying off the debentures, in paying off the mortgage on Battery Road, in paying for North Boat Quay and in the building up of the business". Prospective capital expenditures, conservatively totalling some $1.585 million, desired by London for the acquisition of land and godowns, and the erection or rebuilding of commercial and residential properties, could not be met out of current resources in Singapore. All available funds would be needed for the merchant business (Baddeley, Singapore, to Guthrie & Co., London, S/473 of 2 August 1919).

A month later, Baddeley reported a dramatic change in Singapore's circumstances. The position with the bank had shifted from overdraft to credit balance because of fewer purchases of local produce, on the one hand, and large sales of piece goods on the other. Buyers of imports had not only met their obligations promptly but also had made substantial payments in advance of future purchases. The Singapore money market was very liquid. Money was not being sent to India and China but was flowing into Singapore from those countries because their exchange rates were depreciating while Singapore's was rising:

> *Although the line of argument advanced on page 3 of our letter S/473 is not wrong, it now seems probable that we shall continue easier for funds than we then anticipated — quite apart from the gradual accretion due to the steady income from trading profits.* (Baddeley, Singapore to Guthrie & Co., London, 6 September 1919.)

London then cabled to Singapore expressing concern that the Straits dollar might be appreciated, a very important matter. Singapore replied that there was no prospect of a change in the exchange rate. Pountney, the Colonial Treasurer, was against any appreciation, despite the facts that Thailand had already appreciated its currency and the Netherlands East Indies currency was near melting point. He pointed out that to raise the value of the Straits dollar before the Netherlands East Indies raised the guilder would be suicidal for the Straits as a producer and exporter. Moreover, it was hardly necessary to protect the silver coinage of the Straits since the currency in circulation comprised 93.6% of paper notes and only 6.4% of silver coin (Baddeley, Singapore, to Guthrie & Co., London, 8 September 1919).

Singapore's financial position continued to strengthen, so that by November, Baddeley was proposing investment in local capital works, especially land and godowns. "Such assets would always be readily acceptable collateral for overdrafts or mortgage loans should money be tight in the future" (Baddeley, Singapore, to Guthrie & Co., London, 15 November 1919).

The currency appreciations in India, China, Thailand and Vietnam, from which countries food and other supplies were imported to the S.S., meant that import costs in Straits dollars were always rising. "Exchange alone has caused imports from India, China and Saigon to cost us double or more whereas our exports to the U.K. are not realising any more ... we are suffering with our imports and do not appear to be benefiting with our exports" (Baddeley, Singapore, to Guthrie & Co., London, 22 April 1920). The adverse exchange was damaging not only to trade but also to the local cost of living. The labouring and clerical classes suffered from higher import prices but got little benefit from any rise in export prices. Nevertheless, government remained firmly against any appreciation of the Straits dollar. This was confirmed by the issue of a large, dollar-denominated S.S. Government Loan, which was intended to take up "much of the surplus funds caused by the drift of remittances to the Straits Settlements, which set in from China and elsewhere." The Straits government thus reassured the banks and the public that they did not intend to alter the exchange rate (A. Hood-Begg, London, to Baddeley, Singapore, 28 January 1920).

In this period when money was easy in Singapore it was becoming increasingly tight in London. The Singapore branch was surprised by an unexpected and unadvised drawing by London of £5,783 against Singapore imports. "Rather than you should draw on us would it not be better for us to increase 'free' shipments to you and so save exchange both ways? As we are in funds we shall not be incurring bank interest on overdrafts by so doing" (Baddeley, Singapore, to Guthrie & Co., London, 27 December 1919). London readily agreed and in April 1920 telegraphed for free shipments to relieve financial stringency in London. In May, London also telegraphed for cash remittances totalling £200,000 to cover acceptances falling due.

Singapore then complained that they could not simultaneously meet drafts, remit telegraphic transfers and send free shipments, "Large credits in Singapore will be a thing of the past" (Singapore to London, 26 May 1920). Both sides experienced financial stringency throughout 1920. As trade slowed, London's financial position was "greatly accentuated recently by the extreme dullness which has overtaken the produce market and prevented our disposing of your shipments of produce as they come forward" (London to Singapore, 5 May 1920). London's exports to Singapore were "running between £100,000 and £150,000 a month, against which only £25,000 a month is received … unless you can send free shipments we shall have to call on you for remittances from time to time" (London to Singapore, 3 June 1920). Singapore replied that it would be difficult to meet the deficiency because local trade was stagnant and there was no present hope of increased bazaar collections (Singapore to London, 3 July 1920). Not until the end of the year was there any improvement in Singapore's overstocked position.

At some time in 1920 or 1921, Baddeley left Guthrie & Co., Singapore. His last surviving letter to London No. T/653 is dated 4 June 1920 and headed PRIVATE. Its subject was "Finance" and is of a complaining tone:

As regards the Produce position we note all you write but think you are too ready to put the blame — unfairly — on this end…. What we hope is that advantage was taken of Mr Freeman being in London to go into matters thoroughly with him and that a clear and definite understanding was arrived at for the future conduct of our Produce business. This should certainly have been done…. May we ask that for our guidance your letters be superscribed with the initials of the dictator in accordance with the general custom. (Baddeley, Singapore, to London, 4 June 1920.)

This would not have gone down well with martinet John Anderson; Cunyngham-Brown (1971, p. 246) has Anderson saying, "Baddeley is sacked".

In any event, subsequent private correspondence was between H. Freeman (Singapore) and John Anderson (London). Anderson remained perturbed about finance:

It has already been pointed out that the Capital of G. & Co. is in Singapore, and that any money required on this side must necessarily be sent from Singapore — in some form or another (realizable) — as from time to time it may be required here. This is a basic starting point for our carrying on, and must never be lost sight of by anyone on your side. (John Anderson, London, to H. Freeman, Singapore, 16 September 1920.)

The following month, London sent to Singapore a statement of piece goods finance, in respect of goods delivered or ordered, with a stern covering letter:

... relative to goods contracted for which will have to shipped East, showing the amounts and aggregates of commitments that will have to be financed. The total of these, viz: £461,219 is very startling ... the real and only sound remedy and rectification for the existing situation, lies first in the realization of stocks; and secondly, seeing that no department or branch is ever allowed to use more than its modest and safe proportion of Capital sunk for the time being in stocks. (Anderson, London, to Freeman, Singapore, 28 October 1920.)

A period of tight money in the S.S. caused the Singapore branch to resort to the banks. The Chartered Bank agreed to increase overdraft limit for Singapore to $1 million for the period until 31 March 1921 but would not yet grant a limit of $1.5 million for April to June. The Hong Kong and Shanghai Banking Corporation (HKSBC) reversed an earlier refusal and agreed to provide the £95,000 currently required for telegraphic transfers. Freeman noted that the HKSBC had made no formal demand for title deeds as security but he thought that further increases in the overdraft would probably necessitate it (Freeman, Singapore, to Anderson, London, 20 January 1921).

Anderson replied that "the handing over of the title deeds of any part of the various properties of Guthrie & Co. to any particular bank or creditor is a step that should not be conceded, and to which the Proprietors are absolutely opposed". A good deal of further sermonising followed in this long letter, including "for the good of the firm's credit it must always be said that its assets are not in any way encumbered" and rousingly concluded,

> *The whole question seems to us to be this: does a free and open exami-*
> *nation of the root financial position of Guthrie & Co. Ltd. lead to the*
> *conclusion that if it melted down in the worst possible circumstances,*
> *there is a very large surplus indeed of capital resources? If that question*
> *be answered in the affirmative — and in this connection the mere item*
> *of the value of our stocks is notable — then follows the further question*
> *"Is the business of Guthrie & Co. Ltd. one worthy of giving to it such*
> *further financial accommodation as the present business stress and stag-*
> *nation of sales necessitates?" We do not desire to owe money to anyone.*
> *Our present policy is one of liquidation of our stocks. It is only a matter*
> *of time when this will be accomplished, and the Banks will be paid off.*
> (Anderson, London, to Freeman, Singapore, 17 February 1921.)

The unstated problem was that the firm would not be very sound if stocks were not realisable for cash.

***

The dominant and powerful John Anderson became a partner in Singapore in 1876, was knighted when he finally moved to London in 1912 and controlled the firm from there until shortly before his death on 18 December 1924 (Cunyngham-Brown, 1971, *passim* on most aspects of Anderson's life and career and also on the career of Sir John George Hay and others). Worth special mention is John Emil Taleen in the London office "who knew his job thoroughly, exercised a masterful control over his staff, and who would continue to direct the increasingly important export department — this now being mostly cloths, foodstuffs, tinplate and machinery for Malaya".

The surviving Guthrie papers reveal something of the style, character and competence of several of the firm's other leaders. Of particular interest are the informal reminiscences of staff in Singapore, notably Arthur R. Horne who started with Guthrie & Co. in 1910 at the age of 20 and served nine years in Singapore without any home leave. "The Firm treated me well financially and I resigned with the greatest regret having spent in Singapore and the F.M.S. the happiest years of my life".

Horne's departmental chief for some years was Harry Elphick, a great character whom Horne much admired. Horne was especially grateful to Elphick for moving him in the office from Codes to Imports which was much more his milieu. Elphick had no equal as a Bazaar Man. He had a powerful connection with the leading Chinese dealers and conversed with them in fluent Malay, "He knew their family affairs, business and gambling profits and losses etc." Elphick was also well acquainted with the Sultan of Johore. They had a strong common interest in racing, in which Elphick's participation "was rather officially looked down upon. He was a first rate rider and, although rather big for a jockey, won at Klang and Kuala Lumpur under an assumed name, again because the firm were not enthusiastic". To some extent the firm's disapproval may have been because he was incapacitated for some time after he broke his ribs and a collar bone and sustained head injuries when thrown from a racehorse. The Sultan of Johore was a frequent visitor to Singapore and, as well as their racing chumminess, bought two Daimler cars from Elphick.

A rival to Elphick in Asian society was A.M. Birchall, who was one of several piece goods assistants under H.W. Noon. Birchall could play several musical instruments very well and in that way entertained Chinese dealers in their homes. He lived at Pasir Panjang and at weekends almost like a Malay. Horne said, "I never knew a Guthrie assistant acquire colloquial Malay so quickly as Birchall." In passing, Horne also mentioned admiringly Haji Tahir, a remarkable old man in the office respected by all and often "found praying on his mat in a secluded corner of the Tiffin Room".

The general salary for an assistant began at $200 per month, rising to $300 in yearly increments of $25 a month. Guthries assistants mostly started off living at Kerr's "Leonie House" in Leonie Hill Road. The charge was $75 per month, but better accommodation could be found for $80 per month at Mrs Whitefield's in River Valley Road. Refreshments were cheap — pink gins 10 cents, small whiskies 12 cents with water or 15 cents with soda. Horne recorded that

> *First agreement assistants were expected to join the Cricket Club and the Swimming Club and, if a golfer, Keppel Harbour. On second agreement it was the thing to aspire, but not too soon, to membership of the Ladies Lawn Tennis Club if a good player, and if a good golfer to the Singapore Golf Club. On the third agreement when the old Singaporean began to think of getting married, eyes turned towards the Singapore Club and the Tanglin Club.*

The sociable Governor of the time, Sir Arthur Young, often invited Horne, John Robertson and Arthur Smith, all of Guthries, to play Sunday afternoon tennis with him on the perfect courts at Government House.

A.H. Raeburn, in charge of Codes in London, who had previously served in Singapore had practically all the new assistants through his hands and gave them valuable advice about Singapore. In later times, Raeburn became disgusted with Guthries and several of its staff. He deplored Guthries' promotion of rubber companies at a time when productive capacity was well in excess of demand — flotations merely

> *yield the promoters a good result at the expense of the British public.... I see Malacca Plantations got all the money they wanted easily not withstanding no dividend for two years. J.G. Hay's name [George Hay] appears in big print — pitchforked into position by Sir John [Anderson] after having proved himself unable to keep G. & Co.'s books up to date and after the fiasco in G. & Co.'s securities a/c it is a strange comment on Sir J's assertion that he paid according to value of services.* (Raeburn to Hammond, 6 March 1923.)

In the same letter, Raeburn had harsh words for Bell (a swindler) and Baddeley (feathers own nest).

W.B. (Willie) Cochrane was for many years on Codes and Produce in Singapore and also in charge of local rubber sales. He had worked in London office prior to going to Singapore in 1906. Cochrane was one of the most popular members of staff and his advice and help was always available to new arrivals. Sadly, he died in action in France in 1916. For several years, Cochrane corresponded with A.P. Hammond of Codes in London office. He grumbled about Guthries and had a few digs at George (later Sir John) Hay (incidentally Fred Hammond was friendly with George Hay), and he alluded to the gay life of European bachelors in Singapore.

The many, widespread and pervasive activities described above reveal that the commercial network of Guthries was very extensive and comprised Chinese, Europeans, Malays and Indians in various interlocking ways. These connections were often buttressed by frequent social intercourse among merchants, bankers, government officials and the Asian elites.

***

It is fitting to conclude this chapter with the delightful observations of the Marquis de Beauvoir about Guthrie's Chinese clerks in Singapore in the 1860s:

> *Twenty-five clerks from the Celestial Empire, in white dresses and with their pens stuck behind their ears. They spoke English very passably, went through all the proper formalities with the letter of credit, and wrote their interminable additions in English quite free from error and with the most intense politeness, and a perfect understanding of the whole proceeding.* (*Straits Budget*, 6 April 1939.)

Chapter 8

Merchant Firm 2: Boustead & Co.

In 1828, Edward Boustead came to Singapore from Hong Kong, where he had been engaged in the China trade, to manage the firm of Robert Wise & Co. Boustead founded his own firm in 1830. Correspondence within the firm between its offices in Singapore, Penang and London survives from 1870 and forms the main source for this chapter.

Boustead was a considerable presence in Singapore. He was a leading light in the European commercial community, a founder of the Singapore Chamber of Commerce, the Tanjong Pagar Dock Co., the *Singapore Free Press*, and active in the formation of the Horticultural Society and the Botanic Gardens. He was a noted philanthropist, giving charitably to churches, schools and hospitals. He established the Sailors' Home, originally known as the Boustead Institute, at Tanjong Pagar. Boustead never married while in Singapore but he kept a Malay mistress, Janidah, who bore him four children; one died in infancy but the others were educated in England. When Boustead left Singapore in 1850 he provided Janidah with a house, a plantation and shares in the Tanjong Pagar Dock Co.

In business, Boustead took a partner, Gustave Schwabe, whose cousin formed Sykes Schwabe & Co. in Liverpool. Boustead & Co. exported Straits produce to England while the Liverpool firm sent Piece goods and Rough goods to the East. Boustead & Co. was for a time the agent in Singapore for the Hong Kong and Shanghai Banking Corporation and the Shell Transport & Trading Co. He was very friendly with Tan Kim Seng, a produce dealer with whom he dealt considerably and who looked after Janidah when E.B. left Singapore.

By 1870, Boustead himself had returned to London where he established an office as Edward Boustead & Co., while the Boustead & Co. offices in the Straits Settlements (S.S.) were directed from Singapore. Jasper Young was in charge there until 1873, when he returned to the London office. He was succeeded in Singapore up to 1915 notably by Isaac Henderson, Thomas Cuthbertson, Arthur Young, Bertie Young, T.P. Waddell and E.D. Hewan. In the references that follow, the correspondents will be identified by their initials: Edward Boustead (EB), Jasper Young (JY), Isaac Henderson (IH), Thomas Cuthbertson (TC), Arthur Young (AY), Bertie Young (BY), T.P. Waddell (TPW), E.D. Hewan (EDH); and their locations as: Singapore (S), Penang (P), London (L).

Of the Straits merchant firms, Bousteads probably was the biggest exporter of Straits produce at this early time, 1870 being its best year. Peppers, spices, sugar, sago, hides and rattans were the main items, together with some tin. These were sourced from Chinese dealers in Penang and Singapore.

Produce exports were booming in 1871, especially to America. "We continue to do a very large Am. Business both here and at Penang and we certainly have no reason to complain of bad times" (JY, S, to Davidson, L, 30 May 1871). The large business in produce continued. In August three ships were loaded for America and another 400 tons were awaiting shipment to New York, "I am almost afraid things are too good to last" (JY, S, to EB, L, 26 August 1871). Moreover, the Singapore godowns were full of produce. Singapore declined to send any funds to Penang, where much of the firm's capital was already tied up. The Singapore office bank account was already overdrawn $80,000; the Penang office was told to seek bank credit for its needs. "With the large American business we are doing our Capital is not sufficient" (JY, S, to Stan Young, P, 10 February 1872).

Jasper Young made a most interesting appointment at this time:

I have engaged a son of old Captain Anderson (Shipping Master).... He is about 20 years of age and is now in Colonial Secy's office. He is one of the smartest young fellows in Singapore and we are fortunate in

getting him.... One good thing about engaging young Anderson is that
he looks upon Singapore as his home.... Like Cuthbertson he drinks
nothing stronger than water. (JY, S, to Shaw, L, 18 May 1871.)

The appointee was of course John Anderson who after a short time with
Bousteads was poached by Guthries where his most significant career,
culminating in leadership of that firm, led to riches and a knighthood.

As will emerge in the narrative, the predominant concerns within
Bousteads up to 1920 were, first, Chinese debtors and, second, relations
with European merchant rivals. The latter were sometimes friendly, as in
fixing cartel arrangements and socially, and sometimes fiercely competitive
and distrustful. Young was given also to casting aspersions on the local
Governors and officials. Governor Ord was a "pest", Lieutenant Governor
Anson was "a quiet gentlemanly man, what some would call an amiable old
lady". As for Chief Justice Maxwell, who left Singapore in 1871, "we neither want to see him nor Governor Ord again". On the other hand, Governor
Jervois "is honest and has the welfare of the place at heart".

***

Although Bousteads were a dominant exporter, imports were a very large
element of their business. The import trade was also the main source of
Boustead's constant problems with Chinese dealers who were at the end
of the chain of credit stretching from British manufacturers via merchant
firms to Chinese dealers in the Straits. The credit situation was not helped
by the opening of the Suez Canal which led to every market in the East
being swamped with goods from Europe.

Young expressed concern at "being in the dark" about the financial
position of many dealers. "I am disposed to believe that it would answer
to introduce a cash system here, same as there is in China" (JY, S, to EB,
L, 7 November 1872). Young wanted reform of the credit system but could
not convince other merchant firms. His modest proposal that all imports
be sold at two instead of three months credit found very few supporters in
the Chamber of Commerce. All of the German and most of the British
houses thought three months was correct. It seems that competition was
so fierce that no firm dare move alone and tighter credit terms could be

imposed only with general agreement. Unilaterally, Young wrote that "I have made up my mind for the future only to sell to undoubted men and to give no one more than $20,000 credit" (JY, S, to EB, L, 26 December 1872). At last Young had some modest success when he secured agreement among all importing houses, effective 1 April 1873: not to sell at more than three months credit; to put all PNs through the banks for prompt settlement; not to compromise with bankrupts for less than 50%; to have no further dealings with any debtor who did not pay 75% (JY, S, to Shaw, L, 30 January 1873).

Late in 1873 Young returned to the London office where he worked until 1907. He wrote to Isaac Henderson — his brother-in-law — advising him about handling Chinese dealers. However, the problem of Chinese debtors did not go away. The accumulation of large debts caused the failure also of several of their European creditors in 1872.

A notable failure at this time was Whampoa (Hoo Ah Kay). "It seems that for years past he has been a large speculator in Opium etc., and the man supposed to be well off, if not wealthy, is probably not able to pay more than 50%" (JY, S, to EB, L, 13 July 1872). Whampoa was also the principal partner in Harrison Smith & Co. which "was in a state of hopeless insolvency" (JY, S, to Shaw, L, 20 July 1872). Young had a good opinion of Whampoa, "He is a thoroughly honest old man, but very weak and has allowed himself to be imposed upon by his European friends. On his investments in land and houses I suppose he must have lost nearly $100,000! and by Harrison Smith & Co. $70,000" (JY, S, to Shaw, L, 28 November 1872). Young wrote in similar vein but in more detail to Boustead, noting also that

> when Almeida's failed eight years ago Whampoa bought their shares in Chingtee's Dock for $9000. He has never received a cent of dividend and P.S. & Co. don't value the shares at more than $9000. No doubt the old man was imposed upon. It is a pity in more senses than one that he is in Council — he votes just as he is told by the Governor or P. Simons & Co. (JY, S, to EB, L, 29 November 1872.)

Joshua's were a "frightful failure". "What madness of the Mercantile bank advancing him $535,000 without any security" (JY, S, to EB, L, 7 November 1872). Although in 1870, Velge was deemed "quite safe", by 1872 his firm had failed and he was jailed at the insistence of the

Chartered Bank from which he had borrowed $10,000. Of his other creditors, Gilfillan Wood & Co. were owed $20,000 but got out by fluke as their promissory note was paid 10 days earlier; but Paterson Simons & Co., long overdue, remained unpaid (JY, S, to Shaw, L, 12 October 1872). This Velge was presumably a descendant of John Henry Velge who was born in Malacca in 1796 and died there in 1891. He had for many years lived grandly in Singapore where he was respected and most hospitable. J.H. Velge was a close associate of Jose d'Almeida (Buckley, p. 185) and at some time around 1867 had formed Velge d'Almeida & Co. The younger Velge "was bailed out for $10,000 and afterwards bolted.... It is a pity that such a scoundrel should have got away". In the same letter he informed Shaw that "our losses altogether will amount to about $63,000 which is rather more than our Guarantee a/c here and at Penang amounts to. P. Simons & Co.'s losses amount to close to $70,000" (JY, S, to Shaw, L, 26 December 1872). Nevertheless, Boustead's profits for the half-year to 31 December 1872 were good, with $65,686 to divide among the partners (JY, S, to Shaw, L, 30 January 1873).

In early 1873 the partnership was reconstructed, consequent on the retirement of Stan Young whose share was divided among Boustead, Jasper Young and William Wardrop Shaw. Later Isaac Henderson and Thomas Cuthbertson were admitted to the partnership from 1 January 1874, each getting 10% for the succeeding three years (JY, S, to EB, L, 6 February and 13 March 1873). By November 1873 Jasper Young had returned to London. At this time the character of the export business to America was changing. Rival firms in the Straits were shipping produce to America where Boustead's main client, Cyrus Wakefield, was narrowing his imports to concentrate on rattans, only importing gambier and other cheap dead weight when necessary to fill his rattan ships. Wakefield sought to monopolise the rattan trade; Young sought to please him without alienating other American buyers (JY, L, to IH, S, 12 December 1873 and 23 January 1874). It was important to retain Wakefield's good will. Young offered to lend him up to £20,000 if needed by his firm, and there was instructive correspondence to Cuthbertson in Singapore about treating Wakefield with care (JY, L, to TC, S, 17 April and 11 September 1874) and to Wakefield in Boston (JY, L, to Wakefield, Boston, 24 February, 30 April and 11 September 1874).

In 1874 Young became concerned about the honesty of Ansiang, their Singapore godown keeper, who was suspected of grossly inflating invoices for coolie hire. "The thing is monstrous and some means must be adopted to prevent our being swindled at the rate we are.... Though we did less business in 1873 and 1874 than in 1872 we paid more to Ansiang for coolies — the thing is absurd" (JY, L, to TC, S, 6 November 1874). However, Ansiang survived and when in 1883 he sought to retire, Young beseeched Cuthbertson to try to retain him, "He has been a most loyal and faithful servant and all of us entertain a very warm feeling towards him (JY, L, to TC, S, 2 February 1883).

Jasper Young was close to Cyrus Wakefield and visited him in Boston in June–July 1876. Earlier that year he wrote of "the happy times we used to have in Singapore". While London life was pleasant, there "is nothing in it which comes up to the happy little parties we used to have at each other's houses. I would give a great deal to have the years of my married life in S'pore to live over again" (JY, L, to Wakefield, Boston, 20 April 1876). In the same letter, he observed that 1876 was a bad year for trade. That sentiment was repeated in writing to another American correspondent, noting the "fearful losses" in produce in the last nine months, "All the time I have been in business I have never known things worse than they are now". He added that things had been bad for three years and 1876 would be a very bad year (JY, L, to Fay, USA, 2 May 1876). He also informed Wakefield that Bousteads had several approaches, seeking business, from other American firms. He warned Wakefield that if he declined them, some other firm in Singapore would get the business and "would it not be for your interest that it should be in our hands rather than those of some opponent" (JY, L, to Wakefield, Boston, 6 and 31 May 1876). In the end, however, Bousteads declined the offers from other American buyers.

Young remained in contact with his friend and rival from Singapore days, Adamson (of Adamson Gilfillan and Co., London, and Gilfillan Wood & Co., Singapore). He moaned about German competition, expressed pleasure about honest Governor Jervois and that Adamson and W.H. Read were on the Council. He thought that the Malay States would be best governed if Britain purchased them, as had been done with Penang and Singapore (JY, L, to Adamson, S, 17 May 1876). He also wrote in nostalgic vein to Dr Robert Little in Singapore, on 25 May 1876, saying, "I miss the fun of bargaining with a Chinaman", but his wife would not go back with him.

The issue of cash versus credit sales was perpetual. "I think we must leave it to the S'pore house whether to sell for cash or credit. I have written out to let the Capital stand at $200,000 though I think it is too much, one third of it is locked up in loans, which is not what our Capital was intended for" (JY, L, to Shaw, L, 17 May 1876). In July, he was determined to sell only for cash but by August he realised that such would limit sales severely.

The weak market in Singapore led to more failures. Maclaine Fraser failed in 1876 when old Lewis Fraser withdrew his money from the firm and the junior partners were deemed insolvent. Subsequently, Lewis Fraser was jailed for fraud. A year later Purvis & Co. failed. At this time, the dollar to sterling exchange rate was volatile. At its peak the Straits dollar was about 4s.4d; Young reproved Henderson and Cuthbertson for failing to remit to London at this very favourable rate (JY, L, to TC, S, 29 September 1876). Cuthbertson was urged to stand firm against credit sales in view of wide fluctuations in the exchange rate and Chinese traders being in trouble. Again, Henderson was reproved for missing the high tide of the Straits dollar, "What a glorious chance you had lately and you have missed it. If you had closed with the Bank's offer of £100,000 at 4s.3½d you would have made £10,000" (JY, L, to IH, S, 6 October 1876). Young gave further blasts to Henderson and Cuthbertson in Singapore about mismanagement of exchange and their dilatory approach to American business (JY, L, to IH, S, 27 October 1876 and to TC, S, 3 November 1876). However, produce exports of tin, gambier, pepper, coffee, sugar, hides, sago, tapioca etc., were all booming and Bousteads needed to add to office staff in Singapore (JY, L, to Wakefield, Boston, 14 November 1876).

Young became concerned about "absurd" amounts of money locked up in Penang. "On 30th Sept they had $35,000 lying idle in the Bank while you had not a cent to spare in Singapore" (JY, L, to TC, S, 1 December 1876). At the same time, exchange was up to 4s.5¾d, so Henderson was told to remit as much as possible. He was also informed that his share of the year's profit would be more than £5,000, "perhaps more than any other man in the Straits will make, Cuthbertson excepted"

(JY, L, to IH, S, 19 January 1877). Business continued to boom in 1877, "Our Straits business is perhaps as good now as ever it was. We have been doing very large trade lately in Manchester goods and all for cash" (JY, L, to Fay, USA, 8 March 1877).

Much inter-firm correspondence in 1877 concerned the new share issue by the Tanjong Pagar Dock Co. Young was annoyed at Henderson's failure to resist the share issue idea in Singapore. Young preferred instead that the company raise a sterling loan (JY, L, to IH, S, 27 April and 11 May 1877). In the end, however, Bousteads joined Guthries, McTaggarts and Gilfillans in taking up portions of the Tanjong Pagar Dock issue of new shares (JY, L, to Shaw, L, 5 June 1877). Nevertheless, Young remained dissatisfied with the Tanjong Pagar Dock management. He favoured a regular 12% dividend whereas others wished to limit the dividend rate to 10% in order to conserve money for wharf improvement (JY, L, to IH, S, 26 October 1877). There was also concern about mismanagement of the Eastern & Australian Steamship Co., with which Guthries was associated. It lost half its capital; Boustead and Young had respectively £5,000 and £2,500 invested in it (JY, L, to IH, S, 15 June 1877).

During 1878 there were some tensions within the firm about the allocation of duties and shares in the partnership. In Singapore, Henderson was in charge of Goods and John Cuthbertson of Produce; in Penang, H.W. Gunn was in charge of Goods and John Finlayson of Produce. Young thought the latter pair were the better and praised Gunn for enlarging Penang imports considerably. New partnership shares for the next two years would be E. Boustead 25%, J. Young 25%, I. Henderson 20%, T. Cuthbertson 20%, J. Cuthbertson 10% (JY, L, to TC, S, 12 November 1878). Shaw had withdrawn and consequently Young's finances were strained. "I have had to increase my share of capital by £12,500 and have had to borrow partly to do so" (JY, L, to Wakefield, Boston, 12 July 1879).

***

On 7 April 1879, Jasper Young's wife Maggie (Henderson) died and he was depressed for a time. However, by September he was ardently courting a widow Julia Hannay, whom he married in July 1880. Letters to Wakefield and Fay in America in late 1880 contained praise for the honesty and reliability of Chinese produce dealers and irritation about rival European firms getting into the business of exporting to America (JY, L, to Wakefield, Boston, 23 October 1880).

From the distance of London, Young expressed pessimism about involvement in a tin smelting enterprise in Singapore:

> *Gilfillan's scheme for smelting tin ore is not feasible I think. I am sure it would break down in practice. Better to leave the matter to Chinese. It would give no end of trouble if we took it up. After my experience with T. Pagar I shall have nothing more to do with public companies in S'pore.* (JY, L, to TC, S, 2 January 1881.)

Jasper Young could not have been more mistaken. Mulinghaus and Sword (the latter also a partner in Gilfillan Wood & Co.) started in 1886 in Telok Anson, a port in Perak, as Tin Ore Smelters and General Merchants. In 1887 the business became a limited company, the Straits Trading Co., which has prospered to present times (Yip, 1969, pp. 105–106).

After discussions in London among Boustead, Young, Henderson and Finlayson, a new partnership was formed with those four and T. Cuthbertson, A. Aitken, J. Cuthbertson and H. Gunn in the Straits (JY, L, to TC, S, 24 June 1881). Great dissatisfaction was expressed about the governance of the Tanjong Pagar Dock Co., in which Boustead, Young and Guthrie had major pecuniary interests (JY, L, to TC, S, 8 March 1881). A few months later the Borneo Co. offered to sell their wharf in Singapore and, acting for the Tanjong Pagar Dock Co., Young, Guthrie and Gilfillan made an offer to suit merchant interests. That offer was refused, so Young suggested that discreet negotiations with the Borneo Co. be conducted by Gilfillan or Tidman "who are on good terms with the Directors" (JY, L, to Scott, L, 2 September 1881). This co-operation among merchants was succeeded by a cartel arrangement between Boustead & Co. and Adamson, Gilfillan & Co. such that the two firms would have two-thirds of the shipping business in Singapore. Bousteads hoped also to acquire the agency for the B.I. & N.S. SS Co. (JY, L, to TC, S, 24 November 1882 and 5 January 1883).

Tom Cuthbertson's wife died in childbed and he then returned to England. Finlayson took over as senior partner in Singapore.

Finlayson was soon under fire from Jasper Young. First, there was a rap over the knuckles for Finlayson's tactless letter to Fay (JY, L, to JF, S, 18 January 1884) followed by an apology to Fay for Finlayson's "inexcusable" letter (JY, L, to Fay, USA, 20 January 1884). Then Finlayson's discretionary purchase power was withdrawn because of his reckless speculations in produce (JY, L, to JF, S, 23 January 1884). A few months later, Finlayson received a very stern reproof in a long letter from the London partners, and copied to Thomas Cuthbertson in London (EB, JY and IH, L, to JF, S, 2 April 1884). John Cuthbertson in Singapore was also sent a copy of that letter and told that "we look to you if he deviates from our instructions". Nevertheless, "All of us entertain the most friendly feeling towards him and it rests entirely with himself whether he regains the confidence which through his foolish conduct he has for the present forfeited" (JY, L, to JC, S, 4 April 1884). Five days later, Young wrote again to John Cuthbertson expressing alarm at large unauthorised purchases by Craig and Gunn in Penang and fearing that Craig had reverted to drinking excessively and thus totally unfitted to have charge in Penang (JY, L, to JC, S, 9 April 1884).

Young and Boustead wrote to John Cuthbertson and enclosed a letter of notice for Finlayson. "Take care of it and keep it to yourself in the meantime, and be prepared to seal and deliver it to him on receiving a telegram from us requesting you to do so" (JY and EB, L, to JC, S, 15 May 1884). The letter referred to, signed by Young and Boustead read:

> *As authorised by our Articles of Partnership, we hereby give you notice that your interest in the firms of Boustead & Co. of Singapore and Penang and of Edward Boustead & Co. of London, ceases on the day this Notice reaches your hands. You will be settled with in terms of Clause 15 of said Articles of Partnership.* (JY, L, to JC and JF, S, 15 May 1884.)

Despite all the censure of Finlayson, he was valued by Jasper Young, Tom Cuthbertson and Isaac Henderson, perhaps because his remarkable ability in sales. They would prefer to retain him, noting a better spirit in his recent correspondence. However, Boustead himself had lost confidence in

Finlayson and wished to dismiss him (JY, L, to JC, S, 6 June 1884). Nevertheless, Finlayson was returned to Penang as Tom Cuthbertson returned to Singapore and John Cuthbertson to London.

***

Young was always keen to live harmoniously with other British merchants, especially Gilfillan Wood & Co., so as to lessen competition. "You and they are by far the largest buyers of Produce and, where practicable, it would be well for you to agree as to what prices you should pay" (JY, L, to TC, S, 17 April 1885).

Jasper Young was part of a deputation which "waited upon Lord Derby [Secretary of State for the Colonies] yesterday with regard to the protection of the Straits". They were assured that Singapore would be fully defended by further ships and permanent land defences. However, Penang must be defended by Singapore (JY, L, to TC, S, 1 May 1885).

Serious losses on produce occurred in 1885, in both Singapore and Penang, due to inferior quality and loss of weight, especially in gambier, black pepper, sago flour and tapioca flour (JY, L, to TC, S, 15 May 1885). At the same time, the firm was troubled by failures of Chinese dealers, particularly Eng Cheng & Co., which was very upsetting. Tom Cuthbertson was reproved,

> *How did you come to advance money on Gambier and Pepper that you had not received?… you must on no account advance money on Produce that you have not received…. Gilfillan tells me that his firm never pay for Produce until it has been weighed in their Godowns…. My mind is very uneasy about the lax system in S'pore in giving 1–3 months credit on cash sales. If G.W. & Co., Guthrie & Co., and yourselves could come to some agreement the matter might easily be remedied.* (JY, L, to TC, S, 25 June 1885.)

A few months later, Boustead's cashier in Penang absconded with $40,000. "The pecuniary loss is bad enough … but the disgrace attending it is much worse. The loss through Goan Tye is the greatest disgrace that has ever happened to us" (JY, L, to TC, S, 13 and 20 November 1885).

Finlayson's speculative tendencies continued to cause concern; he was again rapped over the knuckles, and reminded of his reproof two years earlier, for buying 75 tons of white pepper without orders (JY, L, to JF, P, 28 October 1886).

Young was anxious for Tom Cuthbertson to return to London and take charge of the American business in the London office, especially as Henderson had thought of retiring. Young told Tom Cuthbertson that he was uneasy about Finlayson succeeding Tom Cuthbertson in Singapore, "a most valuable man but unfortunately he must be kept in check". Tom Cuthbertson, too, did not escape criticism for allowing credit to Kew Hoe, "If we make a bad debt of $100,000 our character as a firm for prudence is gone" (JY, L, to TC, S, 29 December 1886).

When profits were very high in the second half of 1886, Finlayson rose again in Young's esteem, "It is surprising how Finlayson succeeds in keeping up the profits of the Penang firm and you will please compliment him for me" (JY, L, to TC, S, 7 April 1887). In view of the continued complaints about the poor state of the Produce business, the profits must have originated largely in Imports, where Finlayson was such a good salesman.

Edward Boustead died in 1888. Jasper Young "had been associated with the good old man for 33 years…. The death of our worthy Senior will not affect the business in any way … seeing that we are worth £300,000 or about $1,500,000 I don't think the credit of the firm is likely to be dented" (JY, L, to Fay, USA, 14 April 1888). Jasper Young became the senior partner and Tom Cuthbertson ran the London office.

Finlayson suffered a severe drop in esteem following poor Singapore profits in the first half of 1891. He was sternly reproved for his unfortunate management of Produce through rash speculation. For three half-years in succession the Produce accounts in Singapore came out very badly. Young thought that Finlayson's speculation arose from his anxiousness to get business, "I am convinced that were you to run fewer risks and simply do day-to-day business we would make more money and have, all of us, more peace of mind" (JY, L, to JF, S, 16 September 1891). Young also thought that Finlayson might have too much to do and requested him to resign from the Legislative Council, "Everything points to the necessity of you devoting all your time to the important business interests confided to your care" (JY, L, to JF, S, 18 September 1891). However, there was a repercussion from this advice. Young was

> *pleased to see that you take my remarks in the spirit they were given. I feel sure that if you will simply devote your whole mind to the interests of the business we will have no cause for complaint for the future. Sir Cecil Smith [Governor] wrote to Gilfillan asking him to use his endeavours with us to allow you to retain your seat on the Council but with every desire to meet his wishes we did not see our way.* (JY, L, to JF, S, 27 November 1891.)

The merchant houses established and contributed to the Mactaggart Family Fund, to assist the widow of one of their late colleagues. H.H. The Sultan of Johore also donated £200 and when the fund closed it amounted to over £3,000. Young wrote to the widow to inform her of the fund's closure and its total; in the same letter he added, "Poor W.H. Read is completely cleared out, not a penny left!" (JY, L, to Mrs Mactaggart, 20 May 1892).

The London office was always concerned that the Eastern branches retained the highest possible credit standing,

> *Our credit is of the greatest importance to us and we must do all in our power to maintain it … we are passing through the most trying time I have ever known in business and until things improve we cannot act too cautiously. We had far better lose half a year's profits than have any reflection cast on our name.* (JY, L., to TC, L., 18 June 1892.)

The steady fall of the Straits dollar over 20 years caused a huge fall in the pound sterling value of Tanjong Pagar Dock dividends and in the value of its shares, from £37 to £25 over the two years to December 1892. The Straits dollar fell to 2s.4d in 1893, causing "a loss of about 40% of our capital which we are obliged to keep in silver" (JY, L, to Sandy, India, 8 December 1893). The shares held by Young, Henderson and Tom Cuthbertson dropped some £13,000 in that period. At the same time, Produce profits were shrinking because of very keen competition in the Straits. This led Bousteads to form an agreement, in regard to Penang peppers, with Gilfillan Wood & Co., S.B. & Co., Paterson Simons & Co., which "will I trust put a stop to the intense competition which has been going on in Penang for some years past" (JY, L, to Yeats, P, 23 December 1892). A similar arrangement was intended for sugar.

Merchant co-operation was often sought but not always achieved. In late 1894, Young wrote to Craig in Singapore (Finlayson having returned to London) to emphasise the importance of working harmoniously with Guthries and Paterson Simons (JY, L, to Craig, S, 26 September 1894). Soon afterwards an arrangement was made by Bousteads, Guthries and Paterson Simons regarding the next year's contracts, "I believe the result will still be very good provided you, Anderson [G. & Co.] and Stringer [P.S. & Co.] work harmoniously together ... and see that everything is carried out on the terms of the agreement. It is a splendid business for all three firms concerned and deserves any amount of attention" (JY, L, to Craig, S, 5 October 1894). However, inter-firm harmony was fragile, especially in relations with Guthries:

> *In Anderson you have evidently a very clever and difficult man to do with, and one who if he had his own way would do you no favour ... he will be obliged to act harmoniously with P.S & Co. and yourselves ... the success of this business rests upon all three firms working in concert, both in London and Singapore. On this side there is no fear of trouble but on yours it will require a good deal of judicious management to work smoothly with Anderson.* (JY, L, to Craig, S, 13 February 1895.)

***

Ernest W. Birch, a long-time Straits official, Acting Resident of Selangor, Resident of Negri Sembilan and eventually Resident of Perak, had difficulty living within his income (Thio, 1969, pp. 211–212, summarises Birch's career in Malaya). Young, his Bousteads colleagues and others arranged assistance to Birch totalling $17,200:

> *I positively decline to do anything further. When you come to London it will be necessary for you to execute an Assignment Deed of your Insurance Policy in favour of myself and others.... Is it necessary to return to the East by a P&O str? I daresay I could secure you a passage by one of the Glen steamers at one half the cost of the other.* (JY, L, to Birch, England, 6 March 1895.)

Two years later, with Birch back in the East, Young wrote "When do you propose paying interest on your loan, so long overdue? A good deal of dissatisfaction is expressed by your friends here at the delay and I do think in view of their kindnesses to you when you were in trouble that you should do something quickly" (JY, L, to Birch, Malaya, 9 July 1897). Nine months later, Young sent Birch a reminder and after a further three months wrote again at length,

> *It is very sad your career being spoiled by your financial difficulties, but the remedy is in your own hands. With a moderate amount of self-denial all this may be put right ... why allow your house to be made into a Hotel when Govt allows you only $50 per month for entertaining? You say you cannot help it, but where is your moral courage?*

Young added that Birch's friends in Britain would waive interest due up to 1 January provided Birch would relinquish to them 100 Raub shares which would yield about £400 for debt repayments (JY, L, to Birch, Malaya, 15 July 1898). The matter dragged on for a while. Birch repaid a large part of the loans and Young expressed pleasure at his improved financial position. He also provided a supportive letter for Birch to show to the Governor. Nevertheless he corrected Birch about the amount still owing, "it is £850 instead of £400" (JY, L, to Birch, Malaya, 28 October 1898).

***

Finlayson retired from the firm in November 1896 and Craig was returned to Singapore to take charge of Produce. However, Jasper Young was always worried about Craig's drinking to excess, for which reason he had been sent home to London in January 1896. Young wrote in kindly terms to Finlayson and assured him of future support (JY, L, to JF, S, 8 October 1896).

Arthur Young, Jasper's elder son, was sent to work in Singapore. Jasper Young wrote to him frequently and at length, offering him advice about the business and life "in dear old Singapore where I spent so many happy years" (JY, L, to AY, S, 5 February 1897). Among the tidbits was money to buy a pony and hoping that Arthur Young would exercise it every morning "as I did for 18 years in S'pore" (JY, L, to AY, S, 7 July 1897).

Finlayson joined the Board of the Anglo Egyptian bank, "I got him on through my friend Mr Gwyther of the Chartd. Bank" (JY, L, to Yeats, P, 15 October 1897). Meanwhile, Jasper himself joined the Board of the Chartered Bank (JY, L, to AY, S, 4 February 1898). He turned 65 years of age on 19 April 1898.

A director of the Penang Sugar Estates (P.S.E.) Co. approached Young concerning a rumour that Bousteads intended to go into sugar planting, which might be detrimental to his company. Young reassured him that Bousteads merely intended to form a small company in Penang to produce only basket sugar and be no threat to the P.S.E. Co. This was accepted and furthermore a small investment in the Bousteads venture was promised, together with assistance from Turner, the manager of the P.S.E. Co. On this basis, Young asked Yeats in Penang to "consult with Mr Turner and a few of your Chinese friends, Kim Keng Leong for instance, and take steps to form a company ... Boustead & Co. being the Agents." Young also indicated that Bousteads could subscribe up to £2,000 and that 500 acres would be enough to begin with (JY, L, to Yeats, P, 3 August 1898).

Two days later, Young wrote again to Yeats to report friendly overtures from the Chartered Bank, "I know for a fact that the Bank is willing to do more for B & Co. than any other firm in Penang, and, being a Director, I should like you always to give the Chartered a preference all things being equal" (JY, L, to Yeats, P, 5 August 1898).

Jasper's younger son, Bertie, joined Arthur in Singapore and Jasper dished out two pieces of advice, "I hope you and Arthur go to Church once a day as I regularly did all the 18 years I was in S'pore" and to get on well with the Chinese. "It is a great matter to be popular with them, and never to be angry even when you know they want to swindle you" (JY, L, to BY, S, 19 August 1898).

The Penang sugar venture progressed rapidly, with larger ambitions. The company would be called Straits Sugar Co., it would acquire 1,800 acres of land, capital would be £30,000 of which £20,000 would be issued initially. Sir John Ramsden would take 60% of the shares, Messrs Turner and Pulsford would each have the refusal of 10% and the balance would go to Bousteads; some of that could be allotted to Chinese associates, provided that the Bousteads interest was not less than 15% (JY, L, to Yeats, P, 25 November 1898). Yeats' work on this venture and other things drew uncommon recognition, "Yeats I consider the best man we have in the East" (JY, L, to AY, S, 10 March 1899). However, Yeats was not then in good health. He returned to the UK in 1900 for three months for medical treatment.

The Chartered Bank was by now taking up a good deal of Jasper Young's time but he liked the work. Through his good offices with Phillips Dodge in America the Chartered secured a good share of USA government banking business in Manila (JY, L, to Dodge, Boston, 22 February 1899). Meanwhile, Arthur and Bertie were finding it difficult to live in Singapore within the generous remuneration and benefits provided to them by the firm. Jasper was peeved, "How can you spend so much?" However, in the same letter he expressed warm sentiments about Chinese friends, "Please remember me to Seah Ling Seah. Is Yongsiak of Kuah & Co. still living? One of my best friends when I was in Singapore" (JY, L, to BY, S, 13 October 1899).

E.W. Birch, now rehabilitated financially, was appointed Governor of Labuan and North Borneo from February 1901. On the other hand, "I do not hear a word about a new Governor having been appointed for the Straits. Frank Swettenham would like to get the berth but he won't" (JY, L, to BY, S, 9 November 1900). Jasper was so wrong — Swettenham became Governor of the S.S. in February 1901.

Despite Young giving great credit to Yeats for long good management of Penang, he blamed him for being too easy with advances to some Chinese dealers. While Yeats was in the UK for medical treatment, Greig was sent up to Penang with firm instructions to deal with the debtors. Eng Lee & Co. (tanners) had a large debt, against which Bousteads held the title deeds of the tannery and a $20,000 promissory note signed by Ah Toy and In Yen. Greig was told not to bankrupt the latter two but "you may threaten them as much as you like". Compromise was recommended but further advances were forbidden. Yeo Chin Cheng & Co. surrendered all their assets to Bousteads but Greig was told not to give them a clean discharge. The loss on Ban Seng Huat was to be booked in Bousteads closing accounts, as were the debts of Sir Graeme Elphinstone, Kader Bawa and any others thought doubtful (JY, L, to Greig, P, 13 December 1900). "Altogether I estimate that our losses in Penang will not be less than $80,000!! I must confess that my confidence in Yeats is terribly shaken" (JY, L, to AY, S, 14 December 1900).

Ten months later, when Yeats had returned to Penang, Young agreed to compromise with Chin Guan Huat, Ban Seng Huat and Sin Ban Cheang. He was pleased that most of the debt of Kader Bawa was recoverable. Yeo Chin Cheng was not to be troubled further, in view of his poor health. Elphinstone's account was to be closed as early as possible, without making any undue concession. The most difficult account of Eng Lee & Co. was left to Yeats' discretion, but no further unsecured advances allowed to that firm. Turning to the difficult Tin market, Yeats was told to try to "come to some arrangement with B.M. & Co. and G.W. & Co. whereby the present keen competition might be lessened, but I doubt if this will be possible" (JY, L, to Yeats, P, 4 October 1901).

Young was pleased after Yeats visited the sugar estates of Rubana, Nova Scotia and Gedong and formed favourable impressions. Nevertheless he noted that over £100,000 had been spent on developing the properties and it was time for some return on the outlay (JY, L, to Yeats, P, 29 November 1901). However, the Straits Sugar Co. had cash problems and had run up an overdraft at the Chartered Bank of nearly £20,000 despite an understanding between Young and Yeats that the limit was to be £10,000. Yeats was told that there was to be no further outlay of capital (JY, L, to Yeats, P, 31 July 1902). Nevertheless, the overdraft continued to grow:

> *We shall be glad to know how it is you have allowed the overdraft at the Bank to be increased so enormously without advising us or offering some explanation ... we do not wish you to make any arrangements with regard to coming home. It would never do for you to leave before the affairs of the Straits Sugar Company are put on a satisfactory basis.* (JY, L, to Yeats, P, 2 January 1903.)

At the same time, there was a continued drop in the price of silver. Young was "not sure that cheap silver is not a good thing for the Straits, though it may not suit our books" (JY, L, to Yeats, P, 21 July 1902). Greig in

Singapore was on the receiving end of a "rocket" from Jasper Young over the reluctance of the Singapore branch to cash a draft on Baring Bros:

> *For the future we wish it to be clearly understood that all drafts on Baring Bros. must be cashed at the bank rate without any deduction whatever, and every courtesy should be extended to anyone presenting a Barings credit. Whenever any such person calls he should be at once taken to one of the Seniors. Not many firms have a higher reputation than Boustead & Co. but a few more transactions like the one referred to and it would be gone. How would you like to see the name of our firm erased from the list of Baring Bros. foreign correspondents?* (JY, L, to Greig, S, 16 July 1903.)

By 1904, Young was concerned that too much capital was locked up in godowns. He instructed Waddell to try to sell the Collyer Quay godowns in Singapore for about £50,000 and then lease back the central block for 10–15 years (JY, L, to TPW, S, 15 July 1904). He was also concerned about Boustead's shrinking share of Produce business; he wrote a series of letters to Bertie lamenting Boustead's decline and expressing envy at McKerrow's success. "I look upon his produce business as the best managed in Singapore and ours as the very worst" (JY, L, to BY, S, 29 July 1904). The Singapore profits for the second half of 1904 were disappointing and attributed to heavy losses on Produce due to poor buying and uncovered sales. Notwithstanding these pessimistic views, Bousteads were on the fringe of enjoying great prosperity from involvement in the nascent rubber industry which was about to boom.

In London, Jasper lunched with rival John Anderson of Guthrie & Co. before Anderson returned to Singapore, "While I do not like John Anderson I think it well to keep on good terms with him" and again "Anderson has got a sentimental grievance against B & Co., but it would answer no good purpose to quarrel with him. He is a dangerous man, and we had better keep friends with him if possible" (JY, L, to BY, S, 10 March and 26 May 1905).

A nice testament to British–Chinese commercial relations was Jasper writing that he was "sorry to hear that Eng Hoon is giving up Tin business — we have done business with the firm for over 50 years" (JY, L, to BY, S, 14 July 1905).

Isaac Henderson died on 1 December 1905. Jasper Young was failing. Tom Cuthbertson was running the London office. Finlayson had returned to London. Yeats was in charge in Penang. Singapore was variously in the hands of John Cuthbertson, Craig, Greig and Waddell, while Arthur and Bertie Young were learning the ropes there. The two sons seemingly took time to settle into the business. Arthur suffered from "nervous prostration" for at least 15 months and was absent for some time (JY, L, to Birch, Perak, 25 April 1907).

In 1906, tin was booming and Bousteads were having a good time with that export item. However, Bousteads had lost their former premier position as importers of Manchester goods in Singapore although in Penang they maintained their premier position "doing nearly as much as all the other firms put together" (JY, L, to BY, S, 22 June 1906).

Rubber was on the march. Bousteads hoped to get £80,000 for Rubana estate and, if so, intended to put Nova Scotia estate under rubber. E.W. Birch, now Resident of Perak, helped Bousteads get land grants in that state:

> *I am in hopes that the Company [Straits Sugar] which has already expended about two millions of dollars in Perak will yet become a prosperous concern. Our rubber estates are thriving at a great rate shewing that the land is most suitable. It seems to me not improbable that the Rubber industry not many years hence may exceed in value that of Tin.*
> (JY, L, to Birch, Perak, 25 April 1907.)

Two years later, the Straits Sugar Co. was transformed into Straits Rubber Co. with E.L. Hamilton as chairman. Bousteads had interests in several other estates: Nordanal, Bertam, Malakoff. They also sought subscribers to a private company, Windsor Rubber Estate, near Taiping, in the hope of subsequently floating it as a public company in London.

***

Jasper Young appears to have died in late 1907; the last letter signed personally was dated 28 May 1907 while Bertie signed one on his behalf on 9 July 1907. In 1908, Arthur, in London, recorded the late Jasper's personal assets in the S.S. as: Boustead & Co. share of capital

$30,000; Penang Club Debenture $2,500; shares in Malakoff Estates Penang $18,900. Of course he also left substantial assets in the UK.

Tom Cuthbertson, who had not enjoyed good health since 1906, retired from the firm in 1911. By then, Arthur Young was in command in London and E.D. Hewan in Singapore. Writing privately to Hewan, with copy to Macbain in Penang, Arthur Young said,

> *Mr Cuthbertson ... will, however, continue to serve on the Boards of the various companies with which he is now connected and will also retain his room in this office. Though, therefore, we shall be the poorer by the loss of his active assistance, we shall continue, we hope, to have the pleasure of seeing him from day to day, and no doubt when required the benefit of his advice and experience will be readily placed at our disposal.* (AY, L, to EDH, S, 8 December 1911.)

Tom Cuthbertson had been a strong, reliable and decisive leader in both Singapore and London, and was much valued by the other partners.

Tom Cuthbertson was always worried about the credit of Chinese dealers and debtors. He was alert also to the weakness in Produce business caused by serious shortages of produce and increased competition for it:

> *In the scramble for business, prices, quality and everything else appear to be of no importance as compared with making purchases ... perhaps the most unfavourable feature of all is the starting of a lot of small houses, who are no doubt quite contented if on their business they make a few hundred dollars per month beyond their actual living expenses, and this is a competition which is very hard to work against.* (TC, L, to Greig, S, 12 September 1901.)

He worried too about invasion of the Straits by American business: "The question of Americans being allowed to get control of the S.T. Co. or of the trade in Tin ore in the Native States is a very serious one, not only for us but for the whole colony" (TC, L, to WPW, S, 20 March 1903).

Tom Cuthbertson looked ahead. He saw a future for the Malay States and also thought that the firm should be alert to further developments in the S.S. He wondered if there was opportunity for industrial enterprise in Penang, as "business is getting daily more difficult to do in the old lines" (TC, L, to Yeats, P, 23 January 1902).

Staff costs were a concern, especially the conventional long contracts of up to eight years (five plus three) which made it hard to remove poor performers. "Our intention now in regard to new men is not to make any engagement for a longer term than three years and the question of re-engagement at the expiry of that period will depend entirely on the aptitude shown for business" (TC, L, to Greig, Jago and Yeats, P, 18 February 1902). Also, "there must be a limit to the highly paid Europeans on your staff". And later, "I think all the Singapore firms will have to see what can be done in the way of utilising Eurasians or Chinese for all purely clerical work. Young men from this side costing $200 a month with passages are rather expensive luxuries" (TC, L, to WPW, S, 26 March and 11 September 1903).

Another concern was the rising exchange rate, particularly in view of the $800,000 bank overdraft in Penang and the $486,000 debt of Ee Soon for tin (TC, L, to Macbain, P, 1 May 1903). Greig was reproved for failing to buy sterling when the rate was low. Guthrie & Co. had boldly laid in dollars at low rates, "I really do not understand how it is that with the rise in Exchange from 1/6 to 2/- nothing of similar kind was done in Singapore or Penang … it certainly makes one feel green with jealousy to see that Guthrie & Co. have been so successful in this matter" (TC, L, to WPW, S, 18 September 1903).

At the end of 1903, a new partnership was proposed for the two years 1 January 1905–31 December 1906. Jago would retire and the remaining eight would be J. Young 11½%, A. Young 12%, J.B. Young 12%, R. Craig 8%, R. Yeats 8%, Greig 15%, Waddell 15%, T. Cuthbertson 18½%. It was not deemed possible yet to admit any of the managers (Macbain, Boyd, McKay, Macgregor, Hewan) to partnership but they would each have 2½% of the firm's total profits in addition to their salaries (TC, L, to WPW, S, 10 December 1903).

Waddell had been nominated to the Legislative Council. Tom Cuthbertson approved and advised him to "make the most of your opportunity and try to secure the confidence of the Governor and the Col. Secy. Do your best to get the Indian immigration put on a proper footing and see that T.P. matters are not misrepresented by officials" (TC, L, to WPW, S, 22 March 1904).

In passing, the London offices of eight Straits firms subscribed £100 each for a portrait of Sir Frank Swettenham (TC, L, to WPW, S, 11 December 1903).

***

Arthur Young also saw commercial promise with the opening up of the East coast of Malaya and the consequent likely growth of a Chinese population wanting food and brandy. He thought that if a firm, such as Ann Lock, could be persuaded to establish branches along the East coast they could draw supplies from Bousteads (AY, L, to Gibbons, S, 23 January 1903). Bousteads were also developing a rubber estate in Johore; Arthur wrote to Bertie warning him against over-capitalisation, as had happened in earlier estate ventures (AY, L, to BY, S, 24 August 1904). A similar warning was given to Macbain in Penang concerning the planting of rubber on the Malakoff tapioca estate (AY, L, to Macbain, P, 5 March 1905).

Merchant co-operation was proving difficult. The Borneo Co. Ltd. was accused of infringing a pool agreement about coaling ships, "if a pool is to be a pool I consider that all the members ought to abide most strictly by the conditions" (AY, L, to WPW, S, 10 July 1903). He had taken a set against merchant agreements, "The more I see of these so called agreements, the less do I like them as it is difficult to work harmoniously and, to be candid, I am always rather anxious as to whether they are as strictly adhered to by others as they have been in the past and must be in the future by ourselves". He rejected a proposed agreement among the merchants to increase commissions on imports from 2½% to 5% as likely to lead Chinese dealers to bypass the merchant importers and order supplies directly from the UK (AY, L, to Gibbons, S, 14 April 1905).

Arthur became aware that "Young Ramsden", son of Sir John Ramsden of the Sugar Estates, desired to purchase an estate with rubber on it in an advanced condition. Arthur mentioned the Lowlands Coffee and Rubber Estate to him, and the probable price of $18,000 did not deter him, "his idea apparently is to get an estate which is bearing and producing rubber now with a view to availing himself of the high prices at present available" (AY, L, to By, S, 5 May 1905). Bertie was furnished with particular questions for the present ownership, and urged to pursue a possible transaction speedily. The matter dragged on inconclusively for some time. Arthur passed local opinion from Bertie on to Ramsden, including that Barlow & Co. of Singapore already had an option in hand until the end of July at £83,000 and that another private offer was likely. Arthur added his own note of caution,

> *You must remember that the price of rubber is very high just now and with so much land under cultivation in various parts of the world and a consequent increase in the supply, it appears to me more than probable ... that there will be a heavy decline one of these days. Also there is also the possibility of some chemist discovering a substitute.* (AY, L, to Ramsden, 8 August 1905.)

In the end, Ramsden decided not to purchase. Arthur himself preferred to buy shares in a range of good rubber companies than to sink his money into a particular landed estate.

In response to a request from the Cambridge University Appointment Board (CUAB) about jobs with the agency houses in Malaya, Arthur indicated likely salaries and conditions and that "it would be preferable that the candidate should have been at an English Public School and to a certain extent be proficient in Athletics" (AY, L, to Secy., CUAB, 25 May 1905). In specific relation to an opening in Bousteads, Arthur wrote to Bertie of a man he favoured: 26 years of age, five years business experience in London, educated at Cheltenham and Trinity, Cambridge, played football for the university, threw the hammer and got a rowing Trial Eights Cap, "altogether he is a very nice fellow and could be relied on to work ... you asked me to get you gentlemen and I am getting them for you" (AY, L, to BY, S, 30 May 1905).

Arthur condemned the "bad practice", rife in Eastern ports, of merchants giving financial incentives to ship captains to take on coal from a particular firm. He proposed that the leading firms in Singapore get together to stamp out the practice (AY, L, to WPW, S, 20 October 1905). At this time, anxieties about fixing the exchange rate intensified. In London, Arthur talked with Swettenham who went to fish in the Colonial

Office but found them in a muddle and unwelcoming to his enquiries. "My own private idea is that the only man who could relieve the situation is the Governor and as, to put it mildly, he isn't the right man in the right place, nothing will be done. Really you know I think the man is an old idiot" (AY, L, to Gallwey, S, 26 January 1906). In fact, on 29 January the rate was fixed at 2s.4d to the Straits dollar.

Again, concern arose about Guthrie & Co. in Penang making unfair competition in Hennessey Brandy in order "to take a large share in Penang business for the next two years, no matter whether they make anything out of it or not". Arthur's friend Browning, who ran Hennesseys' business in the Straits, told him that Guthries received only the general trade discount and he could not refuse to supply them if they paid the same price as all the others, "consequently you may take what steps you consider best to compete with Guthries ... but be careful that Chinese dealers not get the best of you by playing Guthries off against you — cute as you are, I have an even higher opinion of Chinese as regards the attribute of cuteness" (AY, L, to Gibbons, P, 4 October 1907).

Fears were expressed that the Homeward Shipping Conference might end because of friction among the members, "I trust this will not happen as free competition is the last thing we want to see" (TC, L, to WPW, S, 18 October 1907).

In late 1907 there was sustained and lengthy correspondence by Tom Cuthbertson in London to Macgregor in Penang and Greig in Singapore concerning speculation in tin by Chinese dealers (TC letters of 18, 25 October and 1, 7, 15, 20 November 1907). Essentially the Chinese sought advances from Bousteads, and other merchant firms, to buy tin ore outputs and hold/carry the stock in anticipation of a rise in tin prices in the London market when supply from the Straits falls off. But to "carry" stock indefinitely could be very expensive because of the interest incurred on the cash advances, let alone the risk of having to sell at a loss if tin prices fell. Cuthbertson sought frequent assurance from Penang about their Chinese debtors: "I shall very glad indeed when all outstandings are closed up and balances settled" (TC, L, to Macgregor, P, 20 November 1907).

At the same time, Bousteads were anxious about the firm's interests in rubber estates. For example, Tom Cuthbertson thought it strange that the Directors of Nordanal estate failed to obtain reserve land from the

Johore government. "In floating a Company this is considered a most important point as we do not anything like such a good price if we have no room for extension (TC, L, to Greig, S, 21 November 1907). It was proposed to float the Singapore and Johore Rubber Co. as a public company, after buying out the ownership of several estates. Capital of £70,000 would be raised for the purpose and Bousteads would be appointed as Singapore Agents and London Secretaries. (AY and TC, L, to Greig, S, 1 November and 13 December 1907). There remained great dissatisfaction about the earlier management of the S & J Rubber Co. in that the interests of that company had been subordinated to those of the predecessor estates (London to Singapore, 14 April 1908).

Tan Jiak Choo of Malacca approached Bousteads with a proposal to float his Pulo Sebang and Sampang Ampah rubber estates as a public company. Interest was shown and Tan was asked for further information (WPW, S, to Tan Jiak Choo, 4 March 1909). However, Bousteads eventually declined the proposal because the properties were scattered over too wide an area and there appeared to be no permanent labour force (AY, L, to Boyd, S, 8 July 1909). Boyd was undertaking the role of a visiting agent and reported generally favourable progress of the Sungei Batu, Malakoff, Rubana and Nova Scotia estates (TC, L, to Boyd, S, 10 December 1909). Meanwhile, Arthur Young had formed the view that for a visiting agent "we ought to have a man of our own to work in conjunction with our Selangor office", and noted that, "G. & Co. Ltd. in conjunction with Malcolm Cumming & Macgregor are starting a business in the F.M.S. [Federated Malay States] … to act as visiting agents" (AY, L, to EDH, S, 22 September 1909).

In similar vein, Arthur contemplated joining interests with the Hampshire brothers with a view to pursuing opportunities in the Malay States as importers, agents for rubber estates and, with the aid of Chinese middleman, buying rubber from Malay smallholder producers (AY, L, to EDH, S, 17 September 1909). Boustead Hampshire & Co. was duly formed and Boyd sent to Kuala Lumpur to get things going. Shortly afterwards, Arthur visited Kuala Lumpur and authorised the purchase of a favourably located office for the new firm in that city (AY, S, to TC, L, 20 January 1910). However, within three years, Arthur learned, confidentially through Tom Cuthbertson at the Chartered Bank, that the bank had advanced some £40,000 to D.W. Hampshire against securities valued at £60,000. Young deprecated the situation and asked Hewan diplomatically to advise Hampshire that he must liquidate the loan as soon as possible (AY, L, to EDH, S, 23 May 1913).

In 1909, there had arisen the question of a contract for the provision of coal for the F.M.S. Railways. Bousteads contemplated making a bid with Paterson Simons & Co., so as to avoid mutual competition and together freeze Gilfillan Wood & Co. out of the business (AY, L, to EDH, S, 18 June 1909).

There was perpetual concern about the debts of Chinese dealers. Lee Ban Hooi owed Bousteads $320,000, while Ban Eng Seng and Gan Teong Teik failed with liabilities of more than $319,000 in which other merchants were also creditors. "It is very disgusting that we should have lost so much money over failures and much of it ought to have been avoided if any reasonable care had been taken by the salesman" (TC, L, to WPW, S, 31 July 1908). The disappointing result for Penang in the first half of 1908 was due largely to defaults or slow payment by Chinese buyers of imports: "we must ask you to see now that limits with each dealer are fixed at a point commensurate with his resources ... common sense and discretion are absolute necessities of dealing with the Penang Chinese" (E. Boustead & Co., L, to Boustead & Co., S, 8 October 1908). However, a subsequent long letter of 1 March 1909 from London to the Penang office warned against becoming too nervous: "easy to get rid of risk by refusing any accommodation to Chinese but you will get rid of your business as well". Yeo Ooi Gark had refrained from making Lee Boon Hooi a bankrupt, on advice from Greig who undertook to make representation to London to let Yeo off the interest on his own debt. "Under these circumstances ... it is of the utmost importance to maintain our reputation for fair dealing with the Chinese. I gave Ooi Gark to understand that if repayment in full of the loan was made before the end of this month, we would forego the whole of the interest" (AY, S, to TC, L, 6 January 1910).

***

On internal matters in that period, Greig intended to retire but was told to tidy up the Chinese speculations in tin first. Staff leave policies were discussed with the Borneo Co. and Paterson Simons & Co.; all three firms agreed on 10 months away on the first leave and eight months away on the second (AY, L, to EDH, S, 10 June 1909). Darke, in the Singapore office, became disappointed at not securing a partnership, as had apparently been intended and expected originally. Arthur felt Darke's disappointment and sought to ease it with a generous percentage of the firm's profits: "we particularly desire that he should be happy and contented and feel that he is being well done by" (AY, L, to EDH, S, 20 January 1915).

External1y, the Government proposed to close the opium farms. Such action would diminish the profits of the Chinese, promote smuggling of *chandu* and lead the Chinese to indulge in spirits: "it is a very serious thing indeed for the Colony to not being able to collect a revenue from opium, considering that 52% of the income comes from that source. I am afraid that public opinion on this side [UK] will force any Government in power to take steps to reduce the consumption of Opium in all our Colonies and Dependencies" (TC, L, to WPW, S, 17 July 1908). Having reflected on the financial and moral sides of the issue, Tom Cuthbertson concluded,

> *I have read with great interest the Governor's Budget. If I could be assured that Morphine and other alkaloids of opium could not be smuggled in, I should view with great satisfaction the extinction of the opium revenue. I am quite sure that the money spent in that article was not only useless but was very harmful to the best interests of the place. If the Chinese do not pay taxes on opium they can afford to pay on other useful articles and trade would benefit, in my opinion, materially, by the disuse of the drug.* (TC, L, to EDH, S, 5 November 1909.)

In 1919, Arthur returned to the East, spending time in Singapore and three weeks in Penang and the F.M.S. While in the neighbourhood of Penang he visited 10 different rubber estates in one week. He found them in good order, especially Chiras: "The Board can go to sleep! Really in beautiful order both as regards cultivation and buildings and labour force who all take off their hats to our Mr Shwabe because they really like him and he looks after them". He took an interest in A.K.E. Hampshire's proposal to float in London the large Kedah rubber estates of Sungei Patani and Bukit Patani. He was attracted to the idea, though fearful that Guthrie & Co. and perhaps Harrison & Crossfield were also interested. He observed, too, that Duncan and Macfadyen were the two biggest rubber men, inspiring confidence and respect all over the peninsula (AY, P, to "My dear Tim", S, 2 May 1919). In Singapore he heard that the Union of Canton Insurance Co. was looking to buy a Singapore property for offices; he indicated that he might consider a sale of Boustead's Collyer Quay property, if the price was right and Bousteads could retain space for its own offices (AY, S, to BY, L, 7 May 1919).

***

This chapter and the preceding one have given inside views of two great British merchant firms, showing their vast outreach and influence. They dominated trade in exports of produce and imports of manufactures. They built strong and mutually beneficial connections with Chinese dealers and investors, and to a lesser extent with Malay sultans and Indian businessmen. They had the ears of Governors and officials in the Straits, the F.M.S. and the Colonial Office in London, in which capacity they assisted relations with the Malay States and facilitated Chinese and Indian immigration.

***

Other important merchant firms, such as Paterson Simons & Co., J.A. Russell and Co., Adamson Gilfillan & Co., have been mentioned in previous pages but no primary records have been found for them. Nevertheless, some fragmentary information is extant for each of these firms and it is appropriate to present it now.

Paterson Simons & Co.

In 1889 the Singapore firm of Paterson Simons & Co. was established as a partnership of William Wemys Ker, William Paterson and Henry Minchin Simons, who had each been engaged in other Singapore firms. In 1867, Thomas Shelford and W.G. Gulland also became partners in

Paterson Simons & Co. which continued under that name after Ker's death in 1874 and the later absorption of Wm. McKerrow & Co. in 1907.

Paterson Simons & Co. was an early exporter of gutta percha, which was used in the manufacture of submarine cables. As well as exports and imports, the firm was interested in shipping, coaling and engineering; it had a controlling interest in the New Harbour Dock Co. until it was expropriated by the S.S. government in 1905. The firm also acted as agents for Malay royalty in Johore until that state accepted a British Adviser in 1914. The various partners were active in the public affairs of the S.S. and several of them, notably Thomas Shelford, served on the Legislative Council. (Unauthenticated brief typescript history of Paterson Simons & Co. provided in 1970 by John H. Morris, a London director.)

J.A. Russell & Co.

J.A. Russell was a son of J.W. Russell who came to Kuala Lumpur around 1890 to be Government Printer. J.A. Russell (J.A.) began his working life around 1897 with the Straits Trading Co. He was already proficient in the Malay language and then took up serious study of Chinese, of which he had learned several dialects from childhood. He was regarded as the finest European scholar of Chinese, speaking fluently in Cantonese, Hokkien, Hakka and Mandarin. In consequence of this linguistic ability and his working association with Chinese mine owners, he was appointed by the Courts to administer the estate of a deceased, rich Chinaman.

In 1904, J.A. formed the firm with his brothers; they had no capital and relied upon loans from their wealthy Chinese friends, including Loke Yew. They became active in the formation of plantation rubber and tea companies before drifting into the role of managing agents of such firms. The Russells speculated very successfully in land, especially along the railway line north from Kuala Lumpur. Among their undertakings were the construction of the magnificent Kuala Lumpur railway station, the development of the Malayan Collieries at Batu Arang and the establishment of the Boh Tea estate in the Cameron Highlands (Information provided orally and in writing in London by T.B. Russell, son of J.A.).

Adamson Gilfillan & Co. (in London) and Gilfillan Wood & Co. (in Singapore)

This firm was founded in Singapore in 1867 by Samuel Gilfillan, William Adamson and H.W. Wood. Its purpose was to export local produce to Britain and in return import textiles and British manufactured goods into Malaya. The export goods were gathered from the Malay archipelago, Bangkok and Saigon, and were graded in Singapore before being packed and shipped to Britain. In conjunction with Mulinghaus, Gilfillan Wood & Co. in 1887 sponsored the formation of the tin smelting company Straits Trading Co. and its Singapore manager, James Sword, left the firm to join the Straits Trading Co. The relationship between Gilfillan Wood and the smelting company was always close.

The Gilfillan Wood & Co. partners were also interested in the formation of the Tanjong Pagar Dock Co. before it was amalgamated with the New Harbour Dock Co. in 1899 and subsequently taken over by the government as the Singapore Harbour Board. As with other leading merchants, several partners of Gilfillan Wood & Co. served on the Legislative Council, notably Sir William Adamson who was knighted for his public service.

In 1904 the Singapore and London businesses were merged into one entity, Adamson, Gilfillan & Co., incorporated in London. The firm remained primarily an export–import enterprise until about 1913 when it first became associated with the rubber industry. It accepted the buying agency for the Goodrich Rubber Co. and undertook the packing of loose rubber; this was done at packing plants in Penang and Perak where the rubber produced on Malay smallholdings was graded and packed for export in substantial quantities until 1920. In the 1930s, Adamson Gilfillan & Co. merged with A.C. Harper & Co. to form Harper Gilfillan & Co. A.C. Harper had been started in about 1886 by Archie Harper who was a trader in Selangor, originally selling horse fodder; but being the only European merchant there at the time he acquired agencies for the Straits Steamship Co. at Klang and of the firm which became Shell Petroleum Ltd. A.C. Harper had merged with another private partnership J.&Q. McClymont & Co. before later forming Harper Gilfillan & Co. (Undated typescript provided by Harper, Gilfillan & Co. Ltd.).

Chapter 9

Finale

These final pages draw together the various threads of British enterprise in the development of the Straits Settlements (S.S.) and the opening up of the Malay States. There was no simple, orchestrated or managed version of British enterprise. Moreover, the British government in Whitehall was extremely reluctant to plant the flag on the Malay peninsula until the late 19th century. The preceding chapters have revealed that the merchants, bankers, governors and administrators were highly individual, as were their organisations. This is not to say that there were never common interests but such had to do with specific events, issues and opportunities; otherwise, differences among the British were commonplace. In so far as there was a British coterie it existed socially, and in each city was centred on the Club, where merchants, bankers and administrators mixed congenially.

Governors and British Officials

The Governors during our period were Harry St. George Ord (1867–1873), Andrew Clarke (1873–1875), William Jervois (1875–1877), William Robinson (1877–1880), Frederick Aloysius Weld (1880–1887), Cecil Clementi Smith (1887–1893), Charles Mitchell (1893–1899), Frank Swettenham (1901–1904), John Anderson (1904–1911), Arthur Young (1911–1919). Of these, the most significant were Ord, Weld and Swettenham, not only for their visionary leadership and administrative abilities but also for their deep sensitivity to Malay interests and to the welfare of the immigrant Chinese and Indians. It should also be obvious that they wished prosperity for all within a free society. Ord was disliked by the established commercial oligarchy in the Straits but was respected by his officials. Weld was generally liked and admired. Swettenham was respected, admired by most but not universally liked.

The Governors were supported by State Residents and other senior officers, notably Hugh Low, Resident of Perak and the model of the residential system. Among very many others of several generations, worthy of mention are Archibald Anson, Henry Belfield, Ernest Birch, Douglas Campbell, Hugh Clifford, Martin Lister, William Maxwell, Walter Pickering, John Rodger and, especially, William Hood Treacher who was Resident in both Selangor and Perak and finally Resident-General of the Federated Malay States (F.M.S.). Clifford had been long-serving in Pahang, first as Agent and later as Resident; he returned to Malaya as Governor S.S. and High Commissioner F.M.S in the 1920s but was then wearied by age. Several of the Governors and their senior officials had prior or later gubernatorial appointments: Ord in Bermuda, Jervois in South Australia and New Zealand, Weld in Western Australia and Tasmania, Anderson in Ceylon, Belfield in Kenya, Birch in North Borneo, Clifford in North Borneo, the Gold Coast, Nigeria and Ceylon, Maxwell in the Gold Coast, Rodger in the Gold Coast and Treacher in North Borneo.

The Governors presided over and generally encouraged substantial public works in the S.S. and the F.M.S. Singapore became a major port for international trade, which was accelerated when the government took over the dock companies and later created the Singapore Harbour Board. The railway system built by government greatly encouraged mining and plantations on the peninsula and yielded good profits to the government. Roads were equally important and Swettenham in particular was dedicated to building roads and pathways. Another government benefit was reform of land laws, accomplished by William Maxwell who had studied the land laws of South Australia. When Maxwell was appointed Commissioner of Lands, S.S. in 1882 he adopted the system of registered title to land, which he later brought to the F.M.S when Resident of Selangor.

In their different ways Ord, Weld, Swettenham and Anderson all advocated and activated the extension of British control in the peninsula. Their effectiveness was helped by their reasonably long tenures as Governors, which led to consistency and stability of policy, and to general confidence in British governance. Although Swettenham served as Governor for only three years, he had spent over 30 years in government service and was the most active expansionist of all.

Free trade was the key to British presence and policy from the beginning. The currency reform of 1906 was undertaken to protect international trade and investment from random fluctuations in the price of silver. Likewise the 1867 transfer from the India Office to the Colonial Office provided local governance and executive power to an extent that gave security and confidence to investment and economic development. Within this settled context, the British administration encouraged and assisted agricultural improvement by Malay smallholders.

Bankers and Financiers

Under the security of British governance, the banks increased in numbers and branch outreach. They benefited from the large deposits made by the expanding governments and they broadened their range of borrowers, especially among the Chinese. With economic development and population growth the exchange and loan business of the banks grew accordingly. There was keen competition between the Chartered Bank and the Hong Kong and Shanghai Banking Corporation, the one well-established in the Straits exchange business and the other backed by resources from its China connections. However, the two banks had a working accommodation and were jointly determined to deter interlopers from their small market in the Straits and the F.M.S.

Major figures in the banking world were C.S. Sherwood, Neave and T.J. Mullins of the Chartered Bank and T.S. Baker of the HKSBC. Sherwood and Mullins as Inspectors were watchful of the soundness and probity of the Chartered's operations in Singapore and Penang. Neave as the long-serving manager in Singapore was most valuable in dealing with Chinese customers as well as with European merchants; the Bank thrived under his management.

The HKSBC had a vigorous Singapore manager in T.S. Baker who was keen on expansion. The Bank moved into Ipoh, Kuala Lumpur, Malacca and Johore Bahru. The F.M.S. government encouraged the ventures in their territories and Johore Bahru was opened to please the Sultan. Baker was a strong proponent of the fixed exchange rate and concerned that the Straits government might weaken on it. Of course a secure fixed rate was greatly to the benefit of the banks in eliminating any risks outside the limited exchange spread set by the gold import and export points. The fixed rate also gave certainty and encouragement to foreign investment flows and thus underpinned economic development.

When business was bad in the Straits, both the HKSBC and the Chartered curtailed advances, sought stronger security for loans and became unwilling to lend against personal guarantees. The Chitty financiers were also very sensitive to fluctuations in trade and exchange, notwithstanding their recourse to funds from India. The Banks and the Chitties were always worried about Chinese speculation in currency (before the 1906 fixed exchange rate) and in commodities, notably tin. The Chinese borrowed directly from the banks and the Chitties, while the latter borrowed from the banks in order to lend to the Chinese. Failures among the Chinese were not infrequent and were doubly damaging.

Merchants

This book began, and will close, with the British merchants. Traders were the original force in the economic development of the S.S. and the Malay States. In their wake came government and banks. The British East India Co. was the first agency of international trade, followed in turn by individual country traders and the merchant firms. The East India Co. also governed, until succeeded by the British India Office and then the Colonial Office.

From the start, the protection and encouragement of international trade was the paramount consideration of government. As trade in the S.S. flourished, the merchants looked further afield into the Malay Peninsula. When the lucrative export trade in tin was threatened in the mid-19th century by factional wars among the Chinese miners and the inability of

Malay rulers to assert control, British authority was introduced on the peninsula to ensure peace and justice and to protect, promote and expand profitable trade and investment. The merchants of the S.S. were most active in urging this intervention.

By the end of the 19th century the trade of British Malaya was most substantial and the British firms were poised for the management of the emergent rubber plantations industry. The major merchant firms were very prominent and powerful within the Straits community. They had formed vocal Chambers of Commerce in Singapore and Penang, while in London the influential Straits Settlements Association was composed largely of retired Straits merchants. In both Singapore and Penang, leading merchants established the newspapers which influenced public opinion. When the S.S. became a Crown Colony in 1867, merchants dominated the non-official membership of the new Legislative Council and caused no end of difficulty to the government and, in particular, to the first Governor of the Colony. Although the Secretary of State for the Colonies inclined towards the Governor's views, the unfortunate Governor Ord found himself sandwiched between merchant interests wishing to rush into the peninsula and the Whitehall government which forbad interference in the Malay States.

The Colonial Office had been fearful of any other European power, especially Germany, encroaching on the Malay Peninsula. The British merchants, however, displayed amiable tolerance of the German merchant community which had been long settled in Penang and Singapore. On the other hand, they were always most worried about Americans getting any foothold in Straits trade.

The merchants generally got along well together, despite their competitive rivalries. They were the major customers of the banks and maintained close relationships with the bankers; for instance John Howard Gwyther of the Chartered Bank got his friend Jasper Young a seat on the Board of the Bank. The most significant merchant personalities during our period were, at different times, Sir John Anderson of Guthries and Edward Boustead of the firm bearing his name. Both were supported and succeeded by long serving staff and partners: A.E. Baddeley and A. Hood-Begg in Guthries; Jasper Young, Tom Cuthbertson and Arthur Young in Bousteads.

Merchant business in the Straits depended crucially on trustworthy relations with the Chinese dealers who provided exportable produce and distributed their imported goods. The successful merchants invariably were close and friendly with Chinese traders, in many cases maintaining long-term business relationships with them and living pleasantly with the Chinese community in general.

***

British enterprise in governance, trade and finance laid the foundations for Singapore and the Federation of Malaya and left each territory in good condition for the successor independent governments. The merchants, bankers and governors should be accorded their due respect.

Bibliography

Allen, G.C. and Donnithorne, Audrey G. (1954) *Western Enterprise in Indonesia and Malaya.* London: Allen & Unwin.

Andaya, B.W. and Andaya, L.Y. (1982) *A History of Malaysia.* London and Basingstoke: Macmillan.

Anson, A.E.H. (1920) *About Others and Myself, 1745–1920.* London: John Murray.

Barlow, Colin. (1978) *The Natural Rubber Industry.* Kuala Lumpur: Oxford University Press.

Barr, Pat. (1977) *Taming the Jungle: The Men Who Made British Malaya.* London: Secker & Warburg.

Bauer, P.T. (1948) *The Rubber Industry: A Study in Competition and Monopoly.* London: Longmans Green.

Begbie, P.J. (1834) *The Malayan Peninsula: Embracing Its History, Manners and Customs of the Inhabitants, Politics, Natural History, etc. from Its Earliest Records.* Madras: Vepery Mission Press.

Bird, Isabella L. (1883) *The Golden Chersonese, and the Way Thither.* Republished 2011. Oxford: John Beaujoy.

Bogaars, G. (1955) The Effect of the Opening of the Suez Canal on the Trade and Development of Singapore. *Journal of the Malayan Branch of the Royal Asiatic Society, 28*(1), March, pp. 99–101.

Buckley, C.B. (1965) *An Anecdotal History of Old Times in Singapore, 1819–1867.* Kuala Lumpur: University of Malaya Press.

Butcher, J. and Dick, H. (eds.) (1993) *The Rise and Fall of Revenue Farming: Business Elites and the Emergence of the Modern State in Southeast Asia.* New York: St Martin's Press.

Cameron, John. (1965) *Our Tropical Possessions in Malayan India.* Oxford in Asia Historical Reprint. Kuala Lumpur: OUP.

Chai, Hon Chan. (1964) *The Development of British Malaya, 1896–1909.* Kuala Lumpur: Oxford University Press.

Chalmers, R. (1893) *A History of Currency in the British Colonies.* London: H.M.S.O.

Chew, Melanie. (2008) *Boustead 1828.* Singapore: Boustead Singapore Ltd.

Chiang, Hai Ding. (1970) Sino-British Mercantile Relations in Singapore's Entrepot Trade, 1870–1915, in J. Ch'en and N. Tarling (eds.) *Studies in the Social History of China and Southeast Asia.* Cambridge: Cambridge University Press.

Collis, Maurice. (1982) *Raffles.* Singapore: Graham Brash.

Courtenay, P.P. (1972) *A Geography of Trade and Development in Malaya.* London: Bell and Sons.

Cowan, C.D. (1961) *Nineteenth Century Malaya: The Origins of British Political Control.* London: Oxford University Press.

Criswell, C.N. (1981) *The Taipans: Hong Kong's Merchant Princes.* New York: Oxford University Press.

Cunyngham-Brown, S. (1971) *The Traders.* London: Newman Neame.

Cunyngham-Brown, S. (1975) *Crowded Hour.* London: John Murray.

Drabble, J.H. (1973) *Rubber in Malaya, 1876–1922.* Kuala Lumpur: Oxford University Press.

Drabble, J.H. (1974) Some Thoughts on the Economic Development of Malaya under British Administration. *Journal of Southeast Asian Studies* 5(2), September, pp. 199–208.

Drabble, J.H. (2000) *An Economic History of Malaysia, c. 1800–1990: The Transition to Modern Economic Growth.* Basingstoke & London: Macmillan.

Drabble, J.H. and Drake, P.J. (1981) The British Agency Houses in Malaysia: Survival in a Changing World. *Journal of Southeast Asian Studies* 12(2), September, pp. 297–328.

Drake, P.J. (1969) *Financial Development in Malaya and Singapore.* Canberra: ANU Press.

Drake, P.J. (1972) Natural Resources *versus* Foreign Borrowing in Economic Development. *Economic Journal* 82(327), September, pp. 951–962.

Drake P.J. (1979) The Economic Development of British Malaya to 1914: An Essay in Historiography with Some Questions for Historians. *Journal of Southeast Asian Studies* 10(2), September, pp. 262–290.

Drake, P.J. (1981) The Evolution of Money in Singapore Since 1819, in *Monetary Authority of Singapore Papers on Monetary Economics.* Singapore: Singapore University Press.

Drake, P.J. (2004) *Currency, Credit and Commerce, Early Growth in Southeast Asia.* Aldershot: Ashgate.

Earl, G.W. (1971) *The Eastern Seas.* Oxford in Asia Historical Reprint. Singapore: Oxford University Press.

Farrell, J.G. (1978) *The Singapore Grip.* London: Book Club Associates and Weidenfeld & Nicolson.

Fielding, K.J. (1955) The Settlement of Penang: By James Scott. *Journal of the Malayan Branch of the Royal Asiatic Society 28*(1), March, pp. 37–51.

Gale, Bruce. (1987) *1837: A 150-Year History of the Malaysian International Chamber of Commerce and Industry.* Kuala Lumpur: The Malaysian International Chamber of Commerce and Industry.

Greenberg, Michael. (1951) *British Trade and the Opening of China, 1800–42.* Cambridge: Cambridge University Press.

Gullick, J.M. (1963) *Malaya.* London: Ernest Benn.

Gullick, J.M. (1983) *The Story of Kuala Lumpur (1857–1939).* Singapore: Eastern Universities Press.

Gullick, J.M. (1992) *Rulers and Residents: Influence and Power in the Malay States, 1870–1920.* Singapore: Oxford University Press.

Gullick, J.M. (1994) *Old Kuala Lumpur.* Kuala Lumpur: Oxford University Press.

Heussler, Robert. (1981) *British Rule in Malaya: The Malayan Civil Service and Its Predecessors, 1867–1942.* Westport, CT: Greenwood Press.

Jackson, J.C. (1968) *Planters and Speculators: Chinese and European Agricultural Enterprise in Malaya, 1786–1921.* Kuala Lumpur: Oxford University Press.

Kaur, Amarjit. (1985) *Bridge and Barrier: Transport and Communications in Colonial Malaya, 1870–1957.* Singapore: Oxford University Press.

Khoo, Salma Nasution. (2006) *More Than Merchants: A History of the German-Speaking Community in Penang, 1800s–1940s.* Penang: Areca Books.

King, F.H.H. (1957) *Money in British East Asia.* London: H.M.S.O.

King, F.H.H. (1988) *The Hongkong Bank in the Period of Imperialism and War, 1895–1918: Wayfoong, The Focus of Wealth.* Cambridge: Cambridge University Press.

Leighton-Boyce, J. (1964) The British Exchange Banks: An Outline of the Main Factors Affecting Their Business up to 1914, in C.D. Cowan (ed.) *The Economic Development of South-East Asia.* London: Allen and Unwin.

Lim, Chong Yah. (1967) *Economic Development of Modern Malaya.* Kuala Lumpur: Oxford University Press.

Loh, Wei Leng *et al.* (2013) *Biographical Dictionary of Mercantile Personalities of Penang.* Penang & Kuala Lumpur: Think City & MBRAS.

Loh, Weng Fong. (1958) *The Singapore Houses of Agency, 1819–1900.* BA (Hons) academic exercise, Department of History, University of Malaya in Singapore.

Lovat, Alice (Lady). (1914) *The Life of Sir Frederick Weld KCMG.* London: John Murray.

Mackenzie, Compton. (1954) *Realms of Silver: One Hundred Years of Banking in the East.* London: Routledge and Kegan Paul.

McIntyre, W. David. (1967) *The Imperial Frontier in the Tropics, 1865–75.* London: Macmillan.

Mills, L.A. (1966) *British Malaya, 1824–67.* Kuala Lumpur: Oxford University Press.

Muirhead, Stuart. (1996) *Crisis Banking in the East: The History of the Chartered Mercantile Bank of India, London and China, 1853–93.* Aldershot: Scholars Press.

Newbold, T.J. (1971) *Political and Statistical Account of the British Settlements in the Straits of Malacca, 1839.* Oxford in Asia Historical Reprint. Kuala Lumpur: Oxford University Press.

Nishimura, S., Suzuki, T. and Michie, R. (eds.) (2012) *The Origins of International Banking in Asia: The Nineteenth and Twentieth Centuries.* Oxford: Oxford University Press.

Ooi, Jin Bee. (1963) *Land, People and Economy in Malaya.* London: Longmans.

Parkinson, C.N. (1964) *British Intervention in Malaya.* Kuala Lumpur: University of Malaya Press.

Rathborne, Ambrose B. (1898) *Camping and Tramping in Malaya.* London: Swan Sonnenschein.

Read, W.H. (1901) *Play and Politics: Recollections of Malaya by an Old Resident.* London: W. Gardner Darton.

Sadka, Emily. (1968) *The Protected Malay States, 1874–1895.* Kuala Lumpur: University of Malaya Press.

Sardesai, D.R. (1977) *British Trade and Expansion in Southeast Asia, 1830–1914.* Columbia, MO: South Asia Books.

Sinclair, Keith. (1967) The British Advance in Johore, 1885–1914. *Journal of the Malaysian Branch of the Royal Asiatic Society 40*(1), pp. 93–110.

Sinclair, Keith. (1967) Hobson and Lenin in Johore: Colonial Office Policy Towards British Concessionaries and Investors, 1878–1907. *Modern Asian Studies 1*(4), pp. 335–352.

Skinner, A.M. (1895) Memoir of Captain Francis Light. *Journal of the Straits Branch of the Royal Asiatic Society* No. 28, August, pp. 1–16.

Spalding, W.F. (1924) *Eastern Exchange Currency and Finance.* London: Pitman.

Stevens, F.G. (1929) A Contribution to the Early History of Prince of Wales' Island. *Journal of the Malayan Branch of the Royal Asiatic Society* 7(3), October, p. 379.

Swettenham, Frank. (1926) Malay Problems, 1926. *British Malaya* 1(1), May, p. 42.

Swettenham, Frank. (1942) *Footprints in Malaya.* London: Hutchinson.

Swettenham, Frank. (1948) *British Malaya.* London: Allen & Unwin.

Tate, D.J.M. (Comp.) (1989) *Straits Affairs: The Malay World and Singapore.* Hong Kong: John Nicholson Ltd.

Thio, Eunice. (1969) *British Policy in the Malay Peninsula, 1880–1910.* Singapore: University of Malaya Press.

Tregonning, K.G. (1965) *The British in Malaya: The First Forty Years, 1786–1826.* Tucson, AZ: University of Arizona Press.

Turnbull, C.M. (1969) The European Mercantile Community in Singapore, 1819–67. *Journal of Southeast Asian History* 10(1), pp. 12–35.

Turnbull, C.M. (1972) *The Straits Settlements 1826–67: India Presidency to Crown Colony.* London: Athlone Press.

Turnbull, C.M. (1977) *A History of Singapore, 1819–1975.* Kuala Lumpur: Oxford University Press.

Webster, Anthony. (1998) *Gentlemen Capitalists: British Imperialists in South East Asia, 1770–1890.* London & New York: Taurus Academic Studies.

Winstedt, R. (1966) *Malaya and Its History.* London: Hutchinson.

Wong, Lin Ken. (1960) The Trade of Singapore, 1819–1869. *Journal of the Malayan Branch of the Royal Asiatic Society* 33(4), pp. 4–315.

Wong, Lin Ken. (1978) Singapore: Its Growth as an Entrepôt Port, 1819–1941. *Journal of Southeast Asian Studies* 9(1), March, pp. 50–84.

Wright, A. and Cartwright, H.A. (1908) *Twentieth Century Impressions of British Malaya.* London: Lloyd's Greater Britain Publishing.

Yip, Yat Hoong. (1969) *The Development of the Tin Mining Industry of Malaya.* Kuala Lumpur & Singapore: University of Malaya Press.

A Note on Sources

In addition to the published works listed in the Bibliography, I have drawn on official, newspaper, journal and private sources.

Official Colonial Office files:

C.O. 273 Straits Settlements, Despatches; C.O. 275 Straits Settlements, Sessional Papers; C.O. 276 Straits Settlements, Government Gazettes; C.O. 425 Straits Settlements, Correspondence; Straits Settlements Annual Reports.

Newspapers and Journals:

The Straits Times, 1876–1913; Journal of the Indian Archipelago and Eastern Asia, 1850–1855; British Malaya, 1926.

Private unpublished papers:

Letter books and reports of Boustead & Co., Guthrie & Co., The Chartered Bank, The Hong Kong and Shanghai Bank. Directors and Senior Executives of these organizations willingly allowed me free access to, and unrestricted use of, their manuscript records. I am especially grateful to Harry Roper-Caldbeck, Trevor Walker and John Wilson who each took considerable interest in my work.

About the Author

Professor Peter Drake, AM
BCom (Hons.1) (Melb), PhD (ANU), DUniv (ACU)

Professor Drake was the founding Vice-Chancellor of Australian Catholic University. His previous academic appointments were in the University of New England, the University of Melbourne and the University of Malaya. Professor Drake has been external examiner in Economics for Universiti Sains Malaysia and The Flinders University of South Australia.

Professor Drake's expertise in international economic development led to roles as a foundation member of the Board of Management of the U.N. Asian and Pacific Development Centre, Kuala Lumpur; member of the steering committee of the ASEAN-Australia Joint Research Project; and Project Manager of Australia's A$15 million Project of Assistance to Institut Pertanian Bogor, Indonesia. He has been a consultant to the World Bank, the Australian International Development Assistance Bureau and AUSAID, and various governments in the Asia-Pacific region.

His period of living in Kuala Lumpur and his many assignments in Southeast Asia have given him a deep understanding of the cultures, history, economies and potential of the region.

Currently, Professor Drake is Chairman of the Academic Board of S.P. Jain School of Global Management (a transnational institution of higher education in Dubai, Singapore and Sydney). He is Chairman of the

Academic Board of the Australian College of Applied Psychology and a Member of Council of Raffles College of Design and Commerce.

Professor Drake has published many articles in academic journals and several books including: *Financial Development in Malaya and Singapore* (1969), *Money, Finance and Development* (1980), and *Currency, Credit and Commerce: Early Growth in Southeast Asia* (2004).

Index

Printed in the United States
By Bookmasters